MILITARY RECORDS, PENSIONS APPLICATIONS, HEIRS AT LAW AND CIVIL WAR MILITARY RECORDS FROM THE FAUQUIER COUNTY, VIRGINIA COURT MINUTE BOOKS 1840-1904

HERITAGE BOOKS
2007

HERITAGE BOOKS
AN IMPRINT OF HERITAGE BOOKS, INC.

Books, CDs, and more—Worldwide

For our listing of thousands of titles see our website
at
www.HeritageBooks.com

Published 2007 by
HERITAGE BOOKS, INC.
Publishing Division
65 East Main Street
Westminster, Maryland 21157-5026

Other books by the author:

Prince William County, Virginia, General Index to Wills, 1734-1951
Fauquier County, Virginia's Clerk's Loose Papers: A Guide to the Records, 1759-1919
Being of Sound Mind: An Index to the Probate Records in Fauquier County Virginia's Clerks Loose Papers and Superior and Circuit Court Papers 1759-1919
The Tax Man Cometh. Land and Property in Colonial Fauquier County, Virginia: Tax List from the Fauquier County Court Clerk's Loose Papers 1759-1782
Military Records, Patriotic Service, & Public Service Claims From the Fauquier County, Virginia Court Minute Books 1759-1784
Military Records, Certificates of Service, Discharge, Heirs, & Pensions Declarations and Schedules From the Fauquier County, Virginia Court Minute Books 1784-1840
Neglected and Forgotten: Fauquier County, Virginia, French & Indian War, Revolutionary War & War of 1812 Veterans

International Standard Book Number: 978-1-888265-99-6

ACKNOWLEDGMENTS

I would like to acknowledge the support and encouragement
to complete this project that I have had from my good friend
and colleague Karen Hughes White and from my husband
Bill Peters. I would also like to thank the staff of the Fauquier
County Public Library and the Fauquier County Circuit Court
for access to the Court Minute Books.

TABLE OF CONTENTS

TABLE OF CONTENTS

INTRODUCTION

1. Historical Introduction

Fauquier County was formed in 1759 from Prince William County. The first Court for the new County was held in May 1759. At that time, Thomas Harrison, having taken the oath and Test required by Parliament, along with the oath as a Justice of the Peace and a Justice of the County Court in Chancery, administered these same oaths and Test to William Blackwell, William Eustace, John Churchhill, William Grant, Yelverton Peyton, Thomas Marshall and George Lampkin. (*Fauquier County Court Minute Books 1759-1763*, <u>May 24, 1759 Court</u>, page 1.)

Once this was done, the Court was "in session" and the official business of the County could begin.

2. The County Court Minutes

The Court Minutes recorded the daily activities of the County Court. These included grand jury presentments and indictments, along with civil and criminal suits, filed as Ended Causes; suits dealings with equity, filed as *Chancery* suits; notices of Land conveyances, like Deeds, Leases, Trusts and Powers of Attorney; records relating to Probate, like the appointment of Administrators and Executors of Estates, Wills, Appraisements, Inventories and Guardianships; records relating to slaves and free Negroes; immigration records in the form of Declarations of Intent and Naturalization; Churchwarden and Overseers of the Poor Apprenticeships and records relating to the Military affairs of the County. All of these documents became part of the Court record.

So too, were records relating to Mills, Bridges and Roads. If a resident wanted to build a mill, he petitioned the Court to erect one. Residents petitioned the Court to open, change, or abandon roads. There are many road petitions for more convenient ways to travel to Mills, to ports like Dumfries or Alexandria, or to the County Courthouse. The County Court regularly appointed Surveyors and Overseers of the roads. These men were charged with the maintenance and repair of the roads in the County. Records relating to Roads, Mills and Bridges make up some of the most interesting reading found in the County Court Minutes and associated papers in the Fauquier County Court Archives.

While this listing is by no matter of mean a complete one, it does show the diverse variety of records recorded in the County Court Minutes.

3. Military Records in the County Court Minutes

One of the most important record groups found in the Court Minutes are records relating to the Military affairs of the County. These records are diverse. Many of them relate to County appointments to the Fauquier County Militia.

There are also food and cash allotments to wives and mothers of soldiers in the Revolutionary establishment. There are Certification of Revolutionary Service and Certificates of Discharge from veterans, Pension Warrants and Declarations. There are innumerable Public Service Claims found through out the Court Minutes. Many of these claims were for beef, pasturage, weapons, horses. Some of these claims dealt with transporting supplies for the army and a few dealt with damage to property from Continental troops in the vicinity.

There are also appointments of patrollers, a quasi-military group of young men appointed to keep an eye on the slave and free Negro community and to keep order in the County.

4. The arrangement of the Military Record base into three volumes: An explanation

I have divided the military records from the Fauquier County Court Minutes into three volumes due to the size of the record base. The first volume deals with records and appointments from 1759-1784. The second volume deals with records from 1784-1840. The third volume deals with records from 1840-1904.

The record break down into the three periods was dictated more by the amount of documentation to be found in the Court Minute Books than from any arbitrary division of dates. The period from the Civil War to 1904, when the County Court went out of existence, does not have a large amount of military record material. I did not want to have two volumes that each contained 150 pages or so and a third volume that contained half that amount. So I determined the dates of inclusion based on the amount of information found in the record base.

5. Fauquier County's Military Records from the Court Minute Books: An Over view

Volume One contains some military records relating to the French and Indian War which ended in 1763 along with the traditional records and appointments made during the Revolutionary War.

Volume Two consists of records relating to Certificates of Heirs at Law of Pensioners and veterans, public service claims, pension warrants and declarations and military appointments. You should be familiar with Pension Law and its impact on the County and on the veteran. It will make the Invalid Pensions and indigent pension declarations much easier to understand.

During the 1820s the pension laws changed every few years. Knowing the changes and how they effected the families of the soldiers will lend insight into the Court process and the certification of heirship found in the County Court Minute books through out that period.

Volume Three includes the military records of the County on the eve of the Civil War. These records furnish insight into the preparations for war as the concept of a United union of states began to break down into a Confederation of independent states. The Court ceased to function once Federal troops occupied the town of Warrenton during the early years of the Civil War.

The records relating to the military after the Civil War dealt with legislative petitions for aid in reconstructing the local infrastructure so that the Court could bring some order into a very chaotic situation. While Fauquier was not a battle ground in the accepted sense of the word, Union troops and commanders made the town of Warrenton their headquarters until the battle of Fredericksburg.

Colonel John S. Mosby and his band of partisan rangers made life difficult for both the federal soldiers and county residents. Federal commanders became increasingly frustrated in their attempt to capture Mosby and continually threatened the citizenry with reprisals.

Most of the military records after 1866 relate to pension applications to the Commonwealth for invalid and/or indigent Confederate soldiers.

6. A word about the types of records found in Volume Three

Many of the traditional military records are found here – County appointments to the Militia, Certificates of Heirs at Law of deceased veterans and pensioners and pension declarations of widows of Revolutionary War and 1812 veterans.

The bulk of the military records after 1866 have to do with certification by the County Court for aid to disabled Confederate soldiers or to their widows. There were several acts for aid passed by the General Assembly which either gave aid for loss of limbs or eyes or commutation money for the same. There were also acts passed to aid the widows of disabled Confederate veterans.

Along with the above mentioned records, Acts were passed to give the County Court and a newly established Confederate Pension Board oversight over the grant of pension money to Confederate veterans. It is extremely useful to know about these various legislative acts as it will help you understand the priorities set by the state government as it grappled with trying to help veterans and their families survive.

I have limited following identified Confederate veterans through the Court records to the County Courts notice that he was exempted from the payment of capitation or other taxes.

7. Some caveats to be aware of...

I have attempted to keep the spelling as it is found in the Court record. Hence, you will find variants of spelling in the record and thus in the index. Be sure to check *all* spelling variations. Remember too that the Clerk of the Court could be innovative and inventive in his rendering of a person's surname and given name.

Many of the Court resolutions and correspondence after the war along with other records have been given verbatim. Others have been summarized. I have *not differentiated between the two* in the Court record narratives.

If you find a record that pertains to an ancestor, you can always request a copy of the Court record from the County Court or make a copy from the Minute Book in question through the State Library or the Fauquier County Public Library. It is *always* desirable to have copies of pertinent records to bolster proof of ancestry for membership in hereditary societies. In many instances, certified copies are required as part of the application papers.

Finally, I have found that errors do sometimes creep into the compilation of narratives dealing with court records, especially in their transition from a research notebook to a computer's word processor. If this should have happened here, I take full responsibility for them. Hopefully, they have been kept to the minimum, thanks to a spell check and a grammar checker incorporated into my word processor. I have used Word 95 to write the narratives associated with these volumes.

Fauquier County Minute Book 1840-1842

October 26, 1840 Court   page 3.
It appears to the satisfaction of the Court that **Jesse Withers, a Pensioner of the United States, died January 7, 1834.** He left as children Elizabeth, who married John Porter; Sarah Alexander and Jesse H. Withers, who are all the children and the heirs and legatees of Jesse Withers at the time of his death.
On the motion of Jesse H. Withers, the same is ordered certified.

February 25, 1840 Court   page 72.
It was proved to the satisfaction of the Court by **Mary Chinn** that she was well acquainted with Enoch K. Withers before the Revolution. Subsequent to that War, Withers married her sister. Mary Chinn lived in Withers' family until his death which happened in 1813, at his residence in Fauquier County.
Mary Chinn then resided with her sister, Enoch K. Withers' widow, until her death in 1829 and since then with her nephew Dr. Thomas T. Withers, son of Enoch K. Withers.
Mary Chinn states that she therefore had it in her power to know the fact that **Enoch K. Withers was an Officer in the Revolution** and that he died testate, leaving the following children: 1) Elizabeth Withers, who married Reverend George Lemmon; 2) Jane Withers, 3) Thomas T. Withers, 4) Mary Withers, who married Dr. Samuel B. Fisher, who resides now in Warren County, Virginia; 5) Horatio C. Withers, who died at his father's late residence in Fauquier County, in May 1840, testate, leaving the following children: Andrew F. Withers, Elizabeth S. Withers, Susan E. M. Withers and Horatio C. Withers, as his only heirs. 6) Alexander S. Withers who now resides in Western Lewis County, Virginia. 7) Robert W. Withers and 8) Edward B. Withers. Both Robert and Edward live in Campbell County, Virginia.
These are Enoch K. Withers' only heirs.
On the motion of Thomas T. Withers, the same is ordered certified to the Register of the Land Office of Virginia.

April 27, 1841 Court   page 112.
On the motion of John Blackwell, the Court orders it certified that satisfactory evidence exhibited to the Court that **Anne Blackwell was a Pensioner of the United States at $320.00 per year.**
She was a **resident of Fauquier County Virginia and died here on December 2, 1840.**

Fauquier County Minute Book 1840-1842

April 27, 1841 Court   page 112. (Cont.)
Heirs of Ann Blackwell, Pensioner of the U.S. and widow of Joseph Blackwell.

   She left the following children: 1) Ann Gaskins, 2) Lucy Smith, 3) Agatha Jeffries, 4) John Blackwell, 5) Wm. Blackwell, 6) James Blackwell, 7) Octavia Chilton, 8) Betsey Edmonds, 9) Jane Blackwell and 10) James Blackwell.
   These are the **children of Joseph Blackwell and the only heirs at law of Ann Blackwell.**

June 30, 1841 Court   page 167.
   On the motion of John Blackwell, the Court certifies that it appears to their satisfaction that **Ann Blackwell, whose administration of estate was granted to John Blackwell on March 24, 1841, was the widow of Joseph Blackwell decd., a Revolutionary Pensioner of the United States.**

September 28, 1841 Court   page 203.
   It was proved to the satisfaction of the Court that **George Purcell, a Pensioner of the United States, died July 20, 1841 in Fauquier County Virginia at his residence. He left no widow.**
   The Court ordered that the above facts be certified to an agent of the United States, for paying pensions in the City of Richmond, Virginia.

September 28, 1841 Court   page 206.
   It appears to the satisfaction of the Court that **David Blackwell, late a Pensioner of the United States, died at his residence in Fauquier County, Virginia on June 25, 1841. He left a widow, Ann Blackwell, who is now alive and resides in Fauquier County.**
   On the motion of Ann Blackwell, the same is ordered certified.

October 25, 1841 Court   page 212.
   On the motion of James Walker, the Court orders it certified that it appears to the Court, by satisfactory evidence, that **Solomon Walker, Sergeant in the Virginia Continental Line in the Revolution, died after 1787, viz. In 1823, intestate.**
   John Walker, Elizabeth Embrey and Susan Burton, children of Solomon Walker were adults and died intestate.

Fauquier County Minute Book 1840-1842

October 25, 1841 Court   page 212. (Cont.)
Notice of Death of Children of Solomon Walker, a Sergeant in the Virginia Continental Line.
The above named are the same persons named in an order made by the Fauquier County Court on March 26, 1840, proving the death of Solomon Walker and his heirs.

October 27, 1841 Court   page 219.
The **Declaration of Hannah Hitt, widow of Peter Hitt, decd.**, taken before Jaquelin A. Marshall, a Justice of this Court, due to her bodily infirmity (she could not attend Court on September 7, 1841) was presented to the Court.
The Declaration was made to obtain a Pension according to the Act of Congress passed July 7, 1838.
Hannah Hitt, about 78, is a resident of Leeds Manor in Fauquier County, Virginia and the **widow of Peter Hitt, a private soldier in the Army during the Revolutionary War.**
Peter Hitt enlisted for 7 years under Captain Elias Edmonds, his enlistment taking place **in 1777. He remained either in the Army or as a prisoner of war until its close when he was released by an exchange of prisoners.**
At the time of his entering the service, Peter Hitt resided in Fauquier County. He was engaged in the Battle of Camden in August 1780 where he was taken prisoner, after being badly wounded and was detained as a prisoner until the aforesaid exchange.
Hannah has often heard her husband, in his lifetime, say that if General Gates had taken Baron DeKalb's advice, and retreated the evening before the battle of Camden, to Ruggler's Mills, that he [Gates] would not have been defeated.
Peter Hitt and his comrades fought over Baron DeKalb until the Cavalry came one them when there were compelled to leave the dead body of their commander.
Peter Hitt owed his life to the chance of getting under a bending tree when the Cavalry charged on them, in which position he was slashed by sword cuts on each of his arms and sides, when he fell, and was afterwards carried, faint and sick, to the enemy's prison ship. It was a long time before he was able to do anything for himself. As soon as he got able to do anything, the British set him to picking ropes.
Hannah Hitt states that she has no documentary evidence in her possession to support this declaration.

Fauquier County Minute Book 1840-1842

October 27, 1841 Court   page 219. (Cont.)
Pension Declaration of Hannah Hitt.

She further states that **she married Peter Hitt in April 1783. Peter Hitt, her husband died on August 31, 1802.** She was not married to him prior to his leaving the service but shortly thereafter. The marriage took place previous to January 1, 1794 at the above stated time. **Hannah was married in the Turkey Run Church in Fauquier County by old Parson Craig** and she has lived in Fauquier County ever since.
      Sworn before J. A. Marshall, Justice.
      (signed) Hannah (x) Hitt   (Seal)

The Court certifies that it has been satisfactorily proven in open Court that Charles Kemper Sr., due to bodily infirmity and unable to attend Court, made the following sworn affidavit before Wm. McCoy, Justice.
      "Charles Kemper Sr. and Peter Hitt enlisted on the same day in August 1777 at Warrenton Virginia for 3 years under Captain Elias Edmonds and marched under Edmonds to Yorktown, in the same mess, until sometime in 1778 when Kemper was discharged by furnishing a substitute and he [Kemper] returned home, leaving Peter Hitt in the service.
      Peter Hitt went with his Regiment to North Carolina and [Kemper] has no doubt that Peter Hitt remained in the service for the whole term for which he enlisted."
      Sworn before Wm. McCoy, Justice. October 28, 1841.

The Court further certifies that affidavit of **Samuel Fisher, a witness, age 76.**
      He was well acquainted with Peter Hitt and Hannah Hitt as far back as 1783. He lived a close neighbor to them for many years and knows they were considered by everybody who knew them as man and wife. **Samuel Fisher did not see them married but heard at the time and has no doubt of the fact that they were married in 1783 by Parson Craig in the Turkey Run Church.**
      Peter Hitt and Hannah Hitt lived near him for about 12 years and had several children. **Parson Craig has been dead many years and the records of Turnkey Run Church as well as the Church itself has long since been destroyed by the lapses of time.**

Fauquier County Minute Book 1840-1842

<u>October 27, 1841 Court</u>   page 219. (Cont.)
Pension Declaration of Hannah Hitt.

The Court further certifies the sworn statement of **Thomas T. Withers**, a Justice of the Court.

He well remembers that **when he was a school boy about 1803 or 1804, the Church Register of the Parish kept by old Parson Craig for Turkey Run Church was in possession of Parson O'Neal, the principal of the Academy in Warrenton near Turkey Run. The Register was torn from time to time and finally destroyed by the boys at the Academy.**

<u>December 28, 1841 Court</u>   page 245.
On the motion of Isham Keith the Court certifies, of its own knowledge that **Isham Keith and James Keith are resident citizens of Fauquier County, Virginia.**

It has been satisfactorily proven to the Court that they are **both brothers of the late Marshall Keith of Columbia County Georgia.**

The Court certifies that it has been fully proven in open Court that **Isham Keith has 2 sons by lawful marriage, who are and have been since their birth, residents of Fauquier County. Isham Keith Jr. an infant, age 8 and James Keith Jr., an infant age about 2** are the only sons of Isham Keith.

The Court further certifies, fully proven in open Court, that **James Keith, the brother as aforesaid of Marshall Keith decd., of Columbia County Georgia, has the following sons by lawful marriage: Thomas A. Keith, age around 27 who is now and has been for some time, a resident citizen of Talledego County, Alabama.**

Another son of James Keith is Marshall Keith, age around 19, a minor, who is now and has been since his birth, a resident of Fauquier County, Virginia.

Thomas A. Keith and Marshall Keith are the only sons of James Keith, brother of Marshall Keith decd., of Columbia County Georgia.

<u>January 24, 1842 Court</u>   page 251.
It was proved to the satisfaction of the Court that **Benjamin Nelson was sole heir at law of Wm. Nelson, a Lieutenant in the Revolutionary War, at the time of Wm. Nelson's death. Ann E. Shutts, wife of Sm. Shutts, is sole heir at law of Benjamin Nelson.**

Fauquier County Minute Book 1840-1842

<u>January 25, 1842 Court</u>   page 251. (Cont.)
Heirs of Wm. Nelson, a Lieutenant in the Revolutionary War.

On the motion of Felix Richards, the same is ordered certified. The Court further certifies that **Benjamin Nelson died intestate**.

<u>April 25, 1842 Court</u>   page 297.
It appears to the satisfaction of the Court, from legal evidence... that **William McClanahan, a Revolutionary Pensioner of the United States, and resident of Fauquier County, died on February 8, 1842, leaving Sarah McClanahan his widow, now a resident of Fauquier County, Virginia**.
The Court ordered the same certified.

<u>October 24, 1842 Court</u>   page 380.
The Court certifies satisfactory evidence exhibited that **Philip Langfit was a Pensioner of the United States** at the rate of $96.00 per year and a resident of Fauquier County. **He died on September 14, 1842 with no widow** at the time of his death.

<u>December 27, 1842 Court</u>   page 406.
The Court certifies that satisfactory evidence was exhibited that **Charles Kemper, a Pensioner of the United States at the rate of $61.33 per year, was a resident of Fauquier County, Virginia. He died in Fauquier County on December 1, 1841. He left a widow, Susannah Kemper.**
On the motion of Charles Kemper Jr. the same is ordered certified.

Fauquier County Order Book 1843-1846

<u>April 1, 1843 Court</u>   page 33.
On the motion of Rice W. Payne, the Court certifies that **William Payne of Fauquier County died on September 19, 1837 in Fauquier County, leaving the following heirs:**
1) Daniel Payne, 2) Fanny Scott, 3) Arthur M. Payne, 4) Ann Green and the children of 5) Marion Clarkson: Milly Clarkson, Henry Clarkson, Marion Clarkson, Wm. Clarkson, John Clarkson, Margaret Clarkson, Ann Clarkson, Betty Clarkson, George Clarkson, Arthur Clarkson and Caroline Clarkson.

Fauquier County Order Book 1843-1846

April 24, 1843 Court   page 35.
The Court certifies that it appears from satisfactory evidence that **Levina Arrowsmith, a Pensioner of the United** States at the rate of $80.00 per year **and a resident of Fauquier County, died in this County on February 2, 1843.**

September 26, 1843 Court   page 102.
On the motion of Betsey Burke, the executrix of Susanna Burk decd., the Court certifies from satisfactory evidence that **Susannah Burk, widow of Wm. Burk, was a Revolutionary Pensioner of the United States at the rate of $80.00 per year.**

She was a resident of Fauquier County Virginia and died in this County on June 23, 1843. She left a will by which she devised all her property of every kind to her daughters Elizabeth, Sally, Fanny and Elizabeth Shaw.

May 27, 1844 Court   page 174.
The Court certifies that satisfactory evidence has been exhibited that **William McClanahan was an invalided Pensioner of the United States at the rate of $48.00 per year.**

He was a resident of Fauquier County and died in this County on February 8, 1842. He left a widow, Sarah McClanahan.

Sarah McClanahan, who has signed the foregoing affidavit and power of attorney **is widow of** the same **Wm. McClanahan**, invalided Pensioner of the United States and deceased as aforesaid.

September 24, 1844 Court   page 220.
On the motion of Solomon Walker, the Executor of Frances Walker decd., the Court certifies that satisfactory evidence has been exhibited that **Frances Walker, widow of Solomon Walker, was a Revolutionary Pensioner of the United States** at the rate of $120.00 per year.

Frances Walker was a resident of Fauquier County Virginia and died here on August 18, 1844, having left a Will devising all her estate of every description to her 3 sons: Samuel Walker, James Walker and Solomon Walker, all of whom are living.

Fauquier County Order Book 1843-1846

March 26, 1846 Court   page 365.

It appears to the Court by satisfactory evidence that **Michael Wiser was a Pensioner of the United States** at the rate of $8.00 per month.

He was a resident of Fauquier County Virginia and died here on April 26, 1846. Michael Wiser left a widow, Nelly Wiser. She has not intermarried since his death but remains his widow.

The Court orders the same certified.

June 23, 1846 Court   page 398.

The Court ordered certified that it was proved to the satisfaction of the court that **Joseph Blackwell entered into the Revolutionary Army as a 2nd Lieutenant in Captain John Chilton's company at the same time his brother John Blackwell entered as a 1st Lieutenant in the same company.**

Captain Chilton was killed at the Battle of Brandywine and John Blackwell was appointed Captain and subsequently taken prisoner at the surrender at Charlestown South Carolina.

Joseph Blackwell, after the Battle of Brandywine, was engaged in the Quartermaster's Department and stationed in Richmond Virginia until the close of the war.

The Court further certified that it was proved to their satisfaction that **Joseph Blackwell died in 1826, testate, leaving the following children as his only heirs: 1) Lucy Smith, wife of Wm. R. Smith; 2) James Blackwell, 3) John Blackwell, 4) Joseph Blackwell, 5) Wm. Blackwell, 6) Agatha Jeffries and 7) Nancy Gaskins, wife of John H. Gaskins.**

One of Joseph Blackwell's heir **Joseph Blackwell died in 1831, testate and of adult age, leaving the following children: 1) Frances Jane Blackwell and 2) James D. Blackwell.**

All of the above heirs reside in Fauquier County.

Octavia E. Chilton, wife of John E. Chilton; and Elizabeth Edmonds, wife of James H. Edmonds, sisters and co-heirs of Frances Jane and James D. Blackwell are now residing in Missouri.

All of which is certified on the motion of John Blackwell, one of the aforesaid heirs.

August 28, 1846 Court   page 424.

The **Pension Declaration of Sarah Strother**, made before B. R. Bradford, Justice of the Peace, was produced before the Court.

The Court orders it certified that satisfactory evidence was produced before the Court that this declaration contains the truth.

Fauquier County Order Book 1846-1849

<u>September 2, 1846 Court</u>   page 2.
The Court ordered it certified that it was proved to the satisfaction of the Court that **Thomas Keith**, late of this County, **was a Captain and Commissary in the Virginia Continental Line from the fall of 1776 to the end of the Revolutionary War.**

Thomas Keith is dead, intestate and has left the following children surviving him as his only heirs: 1) James Keith, 2) Tarleton F. Keith, 3) Isham Keith, 4) Harriet Skinker, now the widow of Wm. Skinker; 5) Mary J. Payne, wife of James Payne and 6) Susan G. James, wife of David James.

Son James Keith has since died, testate, leaving these surviving children: 1) Thomas Marshall Keith, 2) Fanny R. Keith, 3) Mary P. Keith, 4) Susan G. Keith, 5) Judith S. Keith, 6) Harriett S. Keith, 7) Virginia J. Keith, 8) Ritchie R. Keith and 9) Lucy S. Keith as his only heirs at law. James Keith divised all his estate, by will, to his 8 last named children to the exclusion of his sons Thomas and Marshall Keith.

Son Tarleton Keith has since died, in Georgia, intestate, leaving these surviving children: 1) Tarleton F. Keith, 2) Harriet Vance, wife of Wm. Vance, residing in Edgefield District, South Carolina; 3) Judith S. P. Hibler, wife of Isaac A. Hibler, living in Bourbon County, Kentucky. These are his only heirs at law.

Isham Keith, Harriet Skinker, James Payne, Mary J. Payne, David James, Susan G. James and the children of James Keith are all residents of Fauquier and Culpeper County, Virginia.
On the motion of Isham Keith, the Court certifies the same.

<u>January 25, 1847 Court</u>   page 40.
The Pension Declaration of Robert Henson, made under the Act of June 7, 1832, taken before Joseph Thompson and James Payne, Justices of the Peace for this County, was received in open Court and approved and certified to the War Department of the United States.

<u>July 24, 1848 Court</u>   page 310.
The Court ordered it certified that satisfactory evidence was exhibited to the Court that **Annie Claggett, widow of Samuel Claggett, was a Pensioner of the United States** at the rate of $480.00 per year. **She was a resident of Fauquier County, Virginia and died on November 10, 1847** in Fauquier County.

Fauquier County Order Book 1846-1849

<u>July 24, 1848 Court</u>   page 310. (Cont.)
Heirs of Annie Claggett, a Pensioner of the United States and widow of Samuel Claggett.

Annie Claggett left 8 children: 1) Ferdinand Claggett, 2) Christopher Claggett, 3) Thomas Claggett, 4) Anne Bailey, wife of Tomlin Bailey; 5) Elizabeth McCormick, the wife of Thomas McCormick; 6) Cecilia Kirby, wife of John G. Kirby; 7) Sophia Simpson, wife of Thomas Simpson, and 8) Juliet Roach, wife of Robert Roach.

Annie Claggett left **sundry grand children whose names are not known to the Court, some of whom are children of Mary Cooper, decd., daughter of Annie Claggett and her residue to the children of Samuel Claggett decd., son of Annie Claggett. Both Mary Cooper and Samuel Claggett died before their mother Annie Claggett.**

<u>November 30, 1848 Court</u>   page 373.
The Court certified that satisfactory evidence was exhibited before the Fauquier County Court by the oath of Wm. T. Suddoth in open Court, that **James Brown Marshall,** late of Fauquier County, **on or about October 2, 1847 enlisted in the service of the United States for 5 years during the war with Mexico under Lieutenant E. Bradford (then of Richmond, Virginia), 1st Lieutenant, 4th Artillery.**

Marshall entered and remained in the Army and marched to Pueblo in Mexico where he sickened and died on or about March 6, 1848.

<u>January 23, 1849 Court</u>   page 404.
It was proved to the satisfaction of the Court **that William Roe died about the last of 1797 or early in 1798 unmarried,** having first duly made and executed his **will, probated on September 28, 1797.**

Wm. Roe was a **Surgeon's Mate in the Virginia State Navy,** as witnesses always understood, in Roe's family.

He was a **resident of Westmoreland County before and during the Revolutionary War. He removed to Fauquier County where he settled sometime before his death.**

Wm. Roe left the following brothers and sisters: Henry Roe, Bernard Roe, John Roe, Sarah Baker and Elizabeth Tancil.

Fauquier County Order Book 1846-1849

January 23, 1849 Court   page 404. (Cont.)
Heirs of Wm. Roe, a Surgeon's Mate in the Virginia State Navy in the Revolutionary War.

Brother Henry Roe died in Westmoreland subsequent to the death of his brother William Roe. He left these children: 1) James Roe, 2) Winifred Roe, 3) Catherine Roe and 4) Henry F. Roe.
    Brother Bernard Roe died in Culpeper County around 1831 or 1832, unmarried.
    Brother John Roe died in Harrison County, Virginia around 1839 or 1840, leaving these children: 1) Mary McCormick, wife of Wm. McCormick; 2) Sarah Roe, 3) Nancy Roe and 4) Bernard Roe.
    Sister Sarah Baker died around 1816 and since that time her husband Richard has died. She left these children: 1) John Baker, 2) Betsey Baker and 3) Richard Henry Baker (who was named in Wm. Roe's Will); 4) Charles Baker, 5) Alexander Baker, 6) Catharine Baker, 7) Robert Baker and 8) Edward Baker.
    Sarah Baker's son Richard Henry Baker died unmarried under age 21.
    Wm. Roe's sister Elizabeth Tancil died in March 1814, leaving children William Tancil, Susan Tancil, Betsey Tancil and John R. Tancil.

Fauquier County Minute Book 1849-1851

December 24, 1849 Court   page 136.
    The Court hereby certified that satisfactory proof was exhibited before the Court by affidavits of Samuel Chilton and Wm. E. Gaskins, persons entitled to credit that **Elizabeth N. Marshall of Fauquier County is the mother of James B. Marshall, Private in Company A, 4th US Artillery, reported to have died in the United States Service in Mexico.**
    The father of James B. Marshall died some years prior to his son James B. Marshall.
    His mother Elizabeth is now living.
    James B. Marshall died unmarried without issue.

Fauquier County Minute Book 1849-1851

<u>February 25, 1850 Court</u>   page 157.
It has been proved to the satisfaction of the Court that **James M. Marshall decd., the brother of the late Chief Justice of the United States, died on April 26, 1848.**
The Clerk of Court is ordered to certify the same to the Commissioner of Pensions in Washington, D.C.

On the motion of Mary Young, it was proved to the satisfaction of the Court and ordered certified that **the Land Warrant No. 8764 for 13,373 acres of land issued on March 14, 1840 to Mary Young, only heir of Wm. Williams** and which was delivered to Major Edmund Broaddus, as appears by the memo of s. H. Parker, Register of the land Office of Richmond, Virginia **has been casually lost**.

<u>May 25, 1850 Court</u>   page 199.
It was approved to the satisfaction of the Court that **Edward Digges, a Captain in the Virginia State Line in the War of the Revolution, died in 1800.**
On the motion of Thomas E. Digges, Administrator of Edward Digges, the same was ordered certified.

<u>March 26, 1851 Court</u>   page 338.
It was proved to the satisfaction of the Court that **Ann Vowles, a Revolutionary Pensioner of the United States at the rate of $80.00 per year, widow of James Vowles decd., died on March 20, 1851**.
Ann Vowles left the following children: 1) Catharine Lawry, 2) Daniel Vowles and 3) Newton Vowles who are her only living heirs and representatives.

The **Administration of the Estate of Patty Roach decd., the widow of John Roach, was granted to Thomas C. Roach.**

<u>March 26, 1851 Court</u>   page 339.
It was proved to the satisfaction of the Court that **Patty Roach, a Revolutionary Pensioner of the United States at the rate of $68.00 per year, widow of John Roach, died intestate on April 26, 1850**.
She left these children: 1) James M. Roach, 2) John R. Roach, 3) Thomas C. Roach, 4) Robert Roach, 5) Letitia Kemp and 6) Mary McMullin, who are her only heirs at law.

Fauquier County Minute Book 1849-1851

<u>April 28, 1851 Court</u>   page 350.
It was proved to the satisfaction of the Court that **John Catesby
Cocke, formerly of Culpeper County, who was a Captain of Marines
in the Virginia State Navy, died in the lower part of Virginia, after
1807, intestate.**
At the time of John C. Cocke's death, **he resided in** that part of the (then)
County of Culpeper that has since become **Rappahannock County.**

John Catesby Cocke, at the time of his death, **left the following
children as his sole heirs and distributees, surviving him: 1)
Thornton Cocke, 2) Peter Cocke, 3) Alice Edmonds, wife of Elias
Edmonds; 4) --- Cocke who afterwards married Joshua Tennison;
and 5) --- Cocke, who afterwards married --- Fitzhugh.**

**Thornton Cocke removed from Culpeper County Virginia to
Mississippi in 1835 or 1836 and then died, leaving Henry Cocke, his
son as his only surviving heir.**

**Peter Cocke removed from Culpeper County Virginia to Ohio or
Indiana in 1837 or 1838 and died, leaving children whose names and
numbers are not known.**

**Elias Edmonds and wife Alice are dead. Alice died in Fauquier
County Virginia about 1807, leaving daughter Alice Edmonds, now
wife of Alexander Edmonds. They both reside in Fauquier County.**

**Helen Edmonds, who married B. R. Bradford and has since died,
leaving son B. H. Bradford. Her husband [B. R. Bradford] and son
are both living in Fauquier County Virginia.**

**Margaret B. Edmonds, widow of Sydnor Edmonds decd. lives in
Fauquier County. Her son John F. Edmonds is now believed to be
living in Missouri.**

**Joshua Tennison and wife are both dead. Their daughter
Margaret A. Tennison lives in Fauquier and Loudoun Counties,
Virginia; another daughter, who married --- Myers, lives in
Washington, D.C. A son, --- Tennyson, is now a Lieutenant in the
United States Navy.**

**--- Fitzhugh and wife are both dead and her heirs and names are
not known. The heirs are believed to reside in Ohio.**
These children (or descendents) of John Catesby Cocke decd. are his
only heirs and distributees.

Fauquier County Minute Book 1849-1851

April 28, 1851 Court   page 350. (Cont.)
Heirs of John Catesby Cocke, Captain of Marines in the Virginia State Navy in the Revolutionary War.

According to the rules and regulations of the Department of the Interior, in the matter of Settlement of Half-Pay Claims of Virginia, passed by Congress on July 5, 1832, Alice Edmonds, wife of Alexander Edmonds, or husband in right of his wife, are entitled to the Administration of the Estate of John Catesby Cocke decd.
The Court ordered all the same certified.

April 28, 1851 Court   page 353.
It was proved to the satisfaction of the Court that **Hannah Lear, widow of Wm. Lear decd., died on April 20, 1850, intestate.**
Hannah Lear was, at the time of her death, a Pensioner of the United States at the rate of $100.00 per year.
The Court ordered the same certified.

May 26, 1851 Court   page 360.
It was proved to the satisfaction of the Court **that Jane Davis, widow of Wm. Davis, was a Revolutionary Pensioner of the United States** at the rate of $60.00 per year.
Jane Davis died on December 27, 1850, intestate.
The Court ordered the same certified.

June 24, 1851 Court   page 384.
It was proved to the satisfaction of the Court that **Jane Davis, widow** of Wm. Davis, who was a Revolutionary Pensioner of the United States at the rate of $60.00 per year.
Jane Davis died on December 27, 1850 intestate.
She left the **following children as her heirs and her distributees at law: 1) Jane Howison, wife of Stephen Howison; 2) Mary Davis, 3) Susan Chinn, the wife of Henry Chinn; 4) Peyton H. Davis, 5) Isaac F. Davis, 6) Caroline Saunders, wife of Thompson Saunders; 7) Amanda Ayares, wife of Daniel Ayres and 8) Margaret Posey, wife of John Posey.**
All of which the Court ordered certified.

Fauquier County Minute Book 1849-1851

<u>June 26, 1851 Court</u>   page 389.
It was proved to the satisfaction of the Court that **Hannah Lear, widow of Wm. Lear decd., died on April 20, 1850, intestate, leaving James Lear,** her Administrator; **Polly Lear and Nancy Dulin as her only children and heirs at law.**
Hannah Lear at the time of her death was a Pensioner of the United States at the rate of $100.00 per year.
The Court orders all of this certified.

<u>July 28, 1851 Court</u>   page 392.
It was proved to the satisfaction of the Court, by oath of Charles Hunton, age 64, that he was well acquainted with Owen Thomas decd.
Owen Thomas married and settled in Fauquier County Virginia upwards of 50 years ago where he continued to reside until about the year 1828 or 1829 at which time he died.
It was said by **Owen Thomas** and generally understood and believed in his neighborhood that he **came to Virginia from the State of Pennsylvania** and that he had brothers and a sister living there.
Owen Thomas **left the following children: 1) John H. Thomas, 2) Elizabeth Bise, wife of Aaron Bise; 3) Mary Rixey, wife of Samuel Rixey; and 4) Ann H. Rixey, wife of Presley M. Rixey.**
John H. Thomas is now a resident of Fauquier County and is about 50 years old.
Elizabeth Bise, wife of Aaron Bise, died about 30 years ago, leaving one child, Lucelia H. Bise who married John H. Klipstein. Lucelia Bise is over the age of 21.
Mary Rixey, wife of Samuel Rixey, died 9 or 10 years ago, leaving 2 children: Samuel Rixey and Alice Rixey, both of whom are minors.
Ann H. Rixey, wife of Presley Rixey, died 7 or 8 years ago, leaving one child which did not survive its mother but **died a few hours after its birth.**

<u>August 26, 1851 Court</u>   page 401.
It was proved to the satisfaction of the Court that **Susan Deane, widow of John Deane of Fauquier County, Virginia died at the residence of her son in law --- Suddoth on March – 1851.**
Susan Dean had, in January 1851, made declaration to obtain such Bounty Land as she was entitled to, on account of the services of her husband John Deane.

Fauquier County Minute Book 1849-1851

<u>August 26, 1851 Court</u>   page 401. (Cont.)
Heirs of Susan Deane, widow of John Deane.

    **She left the following children as her only heirs at law: 1)
Elizabeth Riley, 2) Robert Deane, 3) Catharine Suddoth and 4)
Thomas Wm. Deane.**

<u>August 28, 1851 Court</u>   page 407.
    It was proved to the satisfaction of the Curt **that John Suddoth died
on December 24, 1850. He had served in a Company, commanded by
Captain Wm. Dulin in the Regiment of Virginia Militia commanded by
Colonel Enoch Rehoe in the War with Great Britain declared by the
United States on June 18, 1812.**
    John Suddoth made and filed his **declaration for** the purpose of
obtaining **Bounty Land** to which h might be entitled for his services.
    When he died, **he left the following children who were, and are,
his only heirs at law: 1) James Suddoth, 2) Wm. Suddoth, 3) Harrison
Suddoth and 4) Frances Putnam.**

<u>September 22, 1851 Court</u>   page 418.
    It was proved to the satisfaction of the Court that **Charles B. Atwell
died on May 13, 1847. At the time of his death, he was a Pensioner of
the United States** at the rate of $70.00 per year.
    He survived his wife and has only one child, Molly Harnett.
    On the motion of Hugh Smith, the Administrator of Charles B. Atwell,
the same was ordered certified.

Fauquier County Minute Book 1851-1853

<u>December 22, 1851 Court</u>   page 4.
    It was proved to the satisfaction of the Court that **Wm. Jett died on
April 23, 1851 and was a Pensioner of the United States** at the rate of
$[illegible] per year.
    He left no widow but the **following children who are his only heirs
at law: 1) Frances C. Rogers, 2) Nancy Settle, 3) Mary M. Rogers, 4)
Wm. Jett and 5) Francis M. Jett.**
    Peter M. Settle is Executor of Wm. Jett. On the motion of the
Executor, the same is ordered certified.

Fauquier County Minute Book 1851-1853

April 26, 1852 Court   page 54.
It appears to the Court, by satisfactory proof, that **Ambrose Walden, late a Pensioner of the United States as a Lieutenant in the Virginia Continental Line, died in Fauquier County in March 1840.**
He left no widow but the following children: 1) Richard Walden, 2) Judith Carter, 3) Wm. Walden and 4) John Walden.
John Walden is the Administrator of the Estate of Ambrose Walden decd.

August 23, 1852 Court   page 112.
It was ordered certified that it was proved to the satisfaction of the Court that **John Farrow, to whom, with Margaret Withers, as the children and only heirs at law of Isaac Farrow, a Land Warrant (No. 27652) was issued from the Department of Interior on August 29, 1852 for 160 acres.**
John Farrow was dead at the date of issuing of the Warrant and **Rosa Farrow, wife of Preston R. Harry of Fauquier County is his daughter.**

August 24, 1852 Court   page 118.
It was ordered certified that it was proved to the satisfaction of the Court that **John Farrow, to whom, with Margaret Withers, as children and only heirs at law of Isaac Farrow decd., a Land Warrant (No. 27652) for 160 acres was issued from the Department of the Interior dated August 29, 1854.**
John Farrow had, at the time of the issuance of the Land Warrant, been absent from the Commonwealth of Virginia and unheard of for more than 7 years successively, having previously resided therein. **According to the Laws of Virginia, such absence is proof of his death.**
The Court, upon such grounds, certifies the death of John Farrow and further certifies that **Rosa Farrow, wife of Preston R. Harry, of Fauquier County, is his daughter and only heir at law.**

August 25, 1852 Court   page 122.
It was proved to the satisfaction of the Court by testimony that **James McCabe, to whom Land Warrant No. 10586 was issued from the Department of the Interior, died intestate on or about May 27th last, without children, leaving a widow Mary McCabe.** [Marginal Note "Baily Coner to pay for this and affixing seal. Marked 'Paid'"]

Fauquier County Minute Book 1851-1853

September 27, 1852 Court   page 143.
     On the motion of **Joseph P. Stigler, one of the heirs at law of James Stigler, decd.**
     It appears to the satisfaction of the Court and hereby certified by the County Court of Fauquier, having probate jurisdiction, that **James Stigler died on or about September 29, 1837.**
     The only heirs at law of James Stigler, who died intestate, are James A. Stigler, Sophia E. Stigler and Joseph P. Stigler, all of whom are 21 years of age.

October 25, 1852 Court   page 158.
     The sworn Declaration **of John Walden, son and administrator of Ambrose Walden decd.** was made in open Court.
"I declared that **my father was a Pensioner of the United States** under and Act of Congress April 1828 up to his death...
     Since his death, **in looking over his papers for the purpose of procuring the Bounty Lands due for the military Services of...**
Ambrose Walden, I have discovered that my father was entitled to an additional pension under an Act of Congress passed in June 1832, he having served more than two years in the War of the Revolution as a Lieutenant.
     The **evidence of this service will appear in the application to the Virginia Legislature for his Bounty Land** as above referred to, which was **granted the heirs of ...Ambrose by an Act of the Virginia Legislature passed at the 1852 session.**
     I fully believe and therefore state that my father did serve more than two years during the Revolutionary War as Lieutenant and consequently is entitled to the benefits of an increased pension provided for such service by the Act of 1832 before referred to.
     (signed)   John Walden

October 25, 1852 Court   page 159.
     The Court ordered certified that **Mary Gunyon, one of the children and heirs at law of Captain Thomas Helm, an officer in the Revolution. Mary and her husband Wm. Gunyon are both dead.**
     Mary, the only child of Mary and Wm. Gunyon, is now the **wife of John Hansbrough of Fauquier County, Virginia.**

Fauquier County Minute Book 1851-1853

<u>October 25, 1852 Court</u>   page 159. (Cont.)
Heirs at Law of Thomas Helm, an officer in Revolutionary Army.

Thomas Helm, another of the children and heirs at law of Thomas Helm, is dead. His only children and heirs at law are Mary Jones, who is now dead, leaving minors Wm. Jones and Ann E. Jones , Wm. M. Helm, Richard P. Helm, Elizabeth Jones, Lena C. Helm, John G. Helm, Margaret Helm, Thomas T. Helm, and James Helm.

<u>March 2, 1853 Court</u>   pages 232-233.
It was this day fully proved in open Court that **Robert E. Peyton, Margaret C. Peyton, John S. Peyton and Richard H. P. Smith are the only heirs at law of Richard H. Peyton, decd., who at the time of his death, was a Captain in the United States Army, having his domicile in this State.**

By an instrument of writing dated July 3, 1846, John S. Peyton transferred and assigned to Robert e. Peyton, for a valuable consideration, all of his right, title and interest in the amount due the estate of Richard H. Peyton for his share in sales of lots in the town of Chattanooga, Tennessee.

Margaret C. Peyton is of full age and a member of the family of Richard E. Peyton.

Richard H. P. Smith is an infant residing with his father in the same neighborhood.

Eliza B. Peyton decd., who was the **mother of Richard H. Peyton,** was in her life time entitled to a distributee share of his estate but that in the adjustments of accounts between her heirs and distributees since her death, her interest in a share of Richard H. Peyton in the proceeds of sales of Chattanooga lots, was transferred to Robert E. Peyton, which is ordered certified.

The Court further certifies that it appears, from the records of this Court, that Robert E. Peyton is the acting administrator of Richard H. Peyton decd., having heretofore on May 26, 1840, duly qualified. He is also the guardian of Richard H. P. Smith.

<u>April 25, 1853 Court</u>   page 271.
It was proved to the satisfaction of the Court and ordered certified that **Churchill Gordon, who died many years since, left the following children** his only heirs and distributees, surviving him:

Fauquier County Minute Book 1851-1853

April 25, 1853 Court   page 271. (Cont.)
Heirs at Law of Churchill Gordon.

1) Wm. S. Gordon, 2) James A. Gordon, 3) Sarah L. Gordon, who married Ludwell Digges; 4) Ann S. Gordon, who married Wm. Blackwell; 5) Eliza L. Gordon who married first, James A. Gordon and second, John H. Digges.

April 25, 1853 Court   page 272.
The **Pension Declaration of Mary Hixon, age 68, resident of Fauquier County, Virginia, for a Pension available to widows of Revolutionary War Pensioners, passed February 3, 1853.**

Mary Hixon is the widow of James Hixon, a Pensioner under the Act of March 1831, the amount obtained due from the Pension up to the death of James Hixon was obtained by George Richards, agent and paid her in 183[-?], being the sum of [left blank]

These papers, to the best of Mary Hixon's knowledge, are filed at Washington, D.C. she further declares she married James Hixon on December 19, 1822.

Her husband died September 4, 1833 at his residence in Loudoun County.

Mary Hixon was not married to him prior to January 2, 1800 but at the time stated above. She is now a widow.

(signed)   Mary Hixon
The Court ordered the same certified.

May 24, 1853 Court
The Court certified that it was proved to its satisfaction that the **heirs at law of Richard Luckett, who died May 29, 1850, are a widow, now surviving [not named], Frederick M. Luckett, Selina E. Seymour, Haywood D. Luckett, Louisa Waller, Adelaide Tolison, David W. Luckett, Robert K. Luckett and Margaret Combs, all of whom are over 21. Two other heirs, Joanna T. Luckett and John R. Luckett, are infants between the ages of 14 and 21.**

May 25, 1853 Court   page 293.
It was proved to the satisfaction of the Court and ordered certified that **Wm. S. Gordon, heir at law of Churchill Gordon is now dead. Philip S. Gordon is his only heir at law.**

Fauquier County Minute Book 1851-1853

<u>May 25, 1853 Court</u>   page 293. (Cont.)
Heirs at law of Churchill Gordon, for services in the Virginia State Navy.

Eliza L. Digges, another heir of Churchill Gordon is now dead and Philip S. Gordon, James A. Gordon, John G. Gordon, Sarah L. Digges and Ann S. Blackwell are the only heirs at law of Eliza L. Digges.
Philip S. Gordon, James A. Digges, John H. Digges, Sarah L. Digges and Ann S. Blackwell are the only heirs at law of Churchill Gordon decd., now living.
They are now the **owners of the Land Warrant issued by the Governor of Virginia, No. 8397 for 2, 666 2/3 acres to the heirs of Churchill Gordon for his services in the Virginia State Navy, which was filed in the General Land Office of the United States on March 12, 1840**.
The Court certifies that the **right of the heirs in the Land Warrant are subject to a ... claim of Ann E. Digges, Sarah G. Digges, Mary A. L. Digges, Portia L. Digges, Catharine R. Digges, Jester A. R. Digges and Jane E. Digges, devisees... of Edward Digges decd. to 1/10 of the land** by virtue of the Contract made between Edward Digges and some of the heirs of Churchill Gordon decd., and the husbands of the others, dated November – 1834.

It was further proved to the satisfaction of the Court and ordered certified that **Edward Digges, one of the heirs (five in number) of Edward (cousin of the Captain) Digges, has died.**
His widow Ann E. Digges, and his daughters Sarah G., Mary A.L., Portia L., Catharine R., Hester A. R. and Jane E. Digges are devisees of the above named Edward Digges. As such, they are entitled to 1/5 of Warrant No. 8585 for 250 acres of land issued by the Governor of Virginia on April 7, 1838 to the heirs of Edward (the cousin of the Captain) Digges and filed in the General Land Office of the United States on July10, 1838.

Fauquier County Minute Book 1851-1853

<u>May 25, 1853 Court</u>   page 293.(Cont.)
Heirs at Law of Thomas Digges relating to Bounty Land Warrant No. 8516.

It was further proved to the satisfaction of the Court and ordered certified that **Dudley Digges, on of the heirs (three in number) of Thomas Digges decd., who was one of the heirs of Edward Digges decd., had died. His widow Judy Digges and children Polly b., Ann Dudley, Lucy and Washington Digges are his only heirs.**
As such **they are entitled to 1/3 of the Bounty Land Warrant No. 8516 for 250 acres of land, issued by the Governor of Virginia on April 7, 1838 to the heirs of Thomas Digges decd. and filed in the General Land Office of the United States on July 10, 1838.**

<u>May 25, 1853 Court</u>   page 295.
It was proved to the satisfaction of the Court and ordered certified that **Henry Fitzhugh is one of the heirs (five in number) of Mary Fitzhugh decd., who was one of the heirs of Edward Digges decd.**
As such, **Henry Fitzhugh is entitled to 1/5 of Bounty Land Warrant #8517 for 250 acres of land, issued by the Governor of Virginia to the heirs of Mary Fitzhugh decd. on April 7, 1838 and filed in the General Land Office of the United States on July 10, 1838.**

<u>June 27, 1853 Court</u>   page 309.
It was proved to the satisfaction of the Court that **Ludwell Digges is one of the heirs at law of Edward (cousin of Captain) Digges.**
As such he is entitled to 1/5 of Bounty Land Warrant No. 8515, issued from the Governor of Virginia on April 7, 1838 and filed in the General Land Office of the United States on July 10, 1838.
Ludwell Digges died in 1836, leaving his widow Sarah L. Digges and children Eliza A. H. Beale, the wife of John G. Beale Jr; Edward Digges, Sarah A. G. Digges, Lucy G. Digges, Churchill G. Digges and Alice P. Digges as his only heirs at law surviving him.
The Court orders all of this certified.

<u>June 27, 1853 Court</u>   page 313.
It was proved to the satisfaction of the Court by Aaron Green and Wm. Dulin, witnesses... that **George Purcell has died. He was issued a Patent by the United States government dated November 6, 1817.**

Fauquier County Minute Book 1851-1853

June 27, 1853 Court   page 313.
Heirs at law of George Purcell, a Revolutionary War Pensioner.

This patent was for a parcel of land therein described. **He has left the following children as his heirs at law: 1) John H. Purcell and 2) Elizabeth Purcell.**
 John H. Purcell is dead. His daughter Mary Purcell of Culpeper County, Virginia is his only heir at law.
 Elizabeth Purcell married Wm. Germans and lives in Fauquier County, Virginia.
 The Court ordered certified that **Wm. Germans and wife Elizabeth and Mary Helen Purcell, the daughter of John H. Purcell, are the only true heirs at law of George Purcell, decd.**

July 26, 1853 Court   page 345.
 The Court certifies that it was proved to its satisfaction that the **heirs at law of Richard Luckett, who died on May 29, 1850, with no widow surviving him are: 1) Frederick M. Luckett, 2) Selina E. Lynn, 3) Haywood D. Luckett, 4) Louisa Waller, 5) Adelaide Talesow, 6) David W. Luckett, 7) Robert K. Luckett, 8) Margaret Combs and 9) Joanna T. Luckett.**
 Joanna T. Luckett is not yet of legal age, having **been born on August 22, 1829. John R. Luckett**, an infant between the ages of 14 and 21, **was born on April 13, 1833.**

August 26, 1853 Court   page 367.
 It was proved to the satisfaction of the Court that the present proprietors of Land Warrants No. 8515, No. 8516, No. 8517 and No. 8518, issued by the Governor of Virginia and dated April 7, 1838 for 250 acres each, was filed in the United States General Land Office at Washington on July 10, 1838.
 The **Land Warrants were issued to the heirs of Edward Digges, Thomas Digges, Mary Fitzhugh and Sarah Fitzhugh respectively** and the persons herein after named.
 Edward Digges left surviving him children and heirs.
 Thomas G. Digges is now living and entitled to 1/5 of Land Warrant No. 8515.

Fauquier County Minute Book 1851-1853

<u>August 26, 1853 Court</u>   page 367. (Cont.)
Heirs at Law of Edward Digges, Thomas Digges Mary Fitzhugh and Sarah Fitzhugh and Proprietor's Rights to Bounty Land Warrants No. 8515, No. 8516, No. 8517 and No. 8518.

Edward Digges is dead, having, by Will recorded in Fauquier County, Virginia, **devised his share to this widow Ann E. Digges and daughters Sarah G. Digges, Mary A. L. Digges, Portia L. Digges Catharine R. Digges, Hester A. R. Digges and Jane Digges** who are now entitled to another fifth of Warrant No. 8515.

Portia Digges is dead, unmarried and without issue and intestate as to the interest in the Warrant.

Sarah D. Digges, widow of Whiting Digges is living and is now entitled to another 1/5 of the Warrant.

Wm. H. Digges is dead, leaving these children and heirs: 1) Catharine Hanney, wife of --- Hanney; and 2) Ann C. Digges, both of whom are now entitled to 1/5 of the Warrant.

Ludwell Digges is dead, leaving children and heirs 1) Edward Digges, 2) Eliza A. H. Beale, wife of John G. Beal Jr.; 3) Sarah E. G. Digges, 4) Churchill G. Digges, 5) Lucy C. G. Digges and 6) Alice P. M. Digges, now entitled to the remaining 1/5 of the Warrant.

Thomas Digges left surviving him these children and heirs: 1) Dudley Digges, dead, who left children and heirs Betty D. Digges, Ann Digges, Lucy Digges, Dudley Digges and Washington Digges. These heirs are now entitled to 1/3 of Warrant 8516.

Lucy B. Fitzhugh is another heir of Thomas Digges and widow of Dudley Digges. She is living and is now entitled to another 1/3 of Warrant No. 8516.

Washington Digges, the third heir of Thomas Digges, is dead. He left children and heirs 1) Francis W. Digges, 2) Catharine R. Digges, 3) Mary C. Digges and 4) Sally H. Matthews, wife of --- Matthews. These children are entitled to the remaining 1/3 of Warrant No. 8516.

Fauquier County Minute Book 1851-1853

<u>August 26, 1853 Court</u>   page 367. (Cont.)
**Heirs at Law of Edward Digges, Thomas Digges Mary Fitzhugh and
Sarah Fitzhugh and Proprietor's Rights to Bounty Land Warrants No.
8515, No. 8516, No. 8517 and No. 8518.**

**Mary Fitzhugh left, surviving her, these children and heirs: 1)
Sarah Thornton, now dead,** who left children and heirs now entitled to
1/5 of Bounty Land Warrant No. 8517. **2) Ann D. Baylor, widow of ---
Baylor, who is living** and entitled to another 1/5 thereof. **3) Henry
Fitzhugh, living** and entitled to another 1/5 thereof. **4) Mary Hunton,
who is dead and leaving children and heirs Lucelia Foster, wife of
Joseph W. foster; and Thomas E. Hunton,** who are now entitled to
another 1/5 of Warrant No. 8517.

**George Fitzhugh who is dead and leaving these children and
heirs: 1) Ellen D. Bowen, wife of Wm. A. Bowen; 2) Ann M. Goodwin,
wife of W.L. B. Goodwin, 3) George Fitzhugh, 4) Susan Vass, wife of
S. M. Vass; 5) Henry Fitzhugh, 6) Rosalie Williams, wife of James
Williams, 7) Thomas Fitzhugh and 8) Betty W. Fitzhugh.** All of these
heirs are now entitled to the remaining 1/5 share of Warrant No. 8517.

**Sarah Fitzhugh left surviving her as children and heirs: 1) Ann H.
Thornton, who is dead and left children and heirs** now entitled to 1/8
of Bounty Land Warrant No. 8518. **2) Elizabeth Cole Gordon, who is
dead and left these children and heirs: Sarah B. Edmonds, widow of
Elias Edmonds decd. and Maria Catlett, widow of --- Catlett decd.**
Both are now entitled to another 1/8 of Warrant No. 8518.
    Other heirs of Sarah Fitzhugh are **3) Edward D. Fitzhugh, 4) Cole
Fitzhugh and 5) Thomas L. Fitzhugh, all of whom are living.** They are
each entitled to 1/8 of Warrant No. 8518. **6) Dudley Fitzhugh, who is
dead, and devised his interest** in Warrant No. 8518, **by Will** recorded in
Fauquier County, Virginia, **to his widow Lucy B. Fitzhugh.** She is now
entitled to the remaining 1/8 of Bounty Land Warrant No. 8518.

    All of which the Court ordered certified to the Commissioner of the
United States General Land Office.

Fauquier County Minute Book 1851-1853

<u>October 25, 1853 Court</u>   page 395.
It was proved to the satisfaction of the Court **that all the children of Wm. H. Digges except two are dead;** A Revolutionary War Bounty Land Warrant No. 8515 was issued to them and others as heirs of Captain Edward Digges. The Land Warrant was issued from the Virginia Land Office and dated April 7, 1838, for 250 acres. It was filed in the United States General Land Office on July 11, 1838.
The remaining living children of Wm. H. Digges are Catharine L. Hanney, wife of --- Hanney and Ann C. Digges. All the other heirs died intestate without issue except for Wm. H. Digges who left surviving him a widow Columbia Digges and a son, Wm. Digges.

Catharine L. Hanney, Ann C. Digges and Wm. Digges are the present proprietors of the share of the children of Wm. H. Digges in Bounty Land Warrant No. 8515.

It was further proved to the satisfaction of the Court that **Laura Fitzhugh, one of the children of George Fitzhugh and heir of Mary Fitzhugh, to who with others, as heirs of Captain Edward Digges,** another Revolutionary War Bounty Warrant No. 8517, for 250 acres was issued, dated and filed as Warrant No. 8515.
Laura Fitzhugh has died intestate and without issue since the Warrant was issued.
The other children of George Fitzhugh, the heir of Mary Fitzhugh, named in Warrant No. 8517, are now all living and are the present proprietors of the share of the heirs of George Fitzhugh in Warrant No. 8517.

<u>October 25, 1853 Court</u>   page 397.
On October 25, 1853, **Elizabeth DeNeal, age 69,** and a resident of Salem, Fauquier County, Virginia, appeared in Court to make the following **Pension Declaration** for a Pension from a Pension Act made February 3, 1853.
Elizabeth DeNeal is the **widow of George DeNeal Jr., a Private in a Troop of Cavalry commanded by Captain Ebin Taylor in – Regiment of Virginia Volunteers or Militia.**
Elizabeth received 5 years half pay on account of the service of her husband 15 or 20 years subsequent and Bounty Land under the Act of September 28, 1850.
For proof of service, reference is made to the papers filed upon which she obtained the half pay and the Bounty Land Warrant.

Fauquier County Minute Book 1851-1853

October 25, 1853 Court   page 397.
Pension Declaration of Elizabeth DeNeal, widow of George DeNeal Jr. a Private in Troop of Cavalry commanded by Captain Ebin Taylor in Regiment of Virginia Volunteers or Militia.

Elizabeth married George DeNeal on May 28, 1806.
Her husband, **George DeNeal Jr. was killed,** as she always understood, **while on parade for battle with the enemy by the wildness of his horse which dashed DeNeal against a tree. He died from that injury in camp.**
Elizabeth DeNeal thinks **his death occurred ...[sometime in] October 1814. She has remained a widow ever since that period.**
On the same day, George E. DeNeal, age 23 and 6 months, came before the Court and declared he is well-acquainted with Elizabeth DeNeale and attested to her statements.

[Note: The Court Minutes state that there is a letter which was to be annexed to the Declaration that gave further evidence to the circumstances surrounding the death of George DeNeal Jr.]

Fauquier County Minute Book 1854-1855

February 27, 1854 Court   page 18.
The Court certifies that it has been satisfactorily proven this day in open Court that **Dr. Gustavus B. Horner, a Surgeon's Mate in the Revolutionary Army, died in Fauquier County Virginia about the year 1815.**
He **left a widow who is since deceased and the following children and heirs:**
Francis Whiting, then married, but now a widow.

Elizabeth Horner, who married Thomas L. Moore. Elizabeth Moore is since dead, leaving an only son and heir Richard H. Moore. Richard H. Moore died intestate, leaving as his heir at law his father Thomas L. Moore.

Catharine J. Marr, the widow of John Marr.

Fauquier County Minute Book 1854-1855

<u>February 27, 1854 Court</u>   page 18. (Cont.)
Heirs at law of Gustuvus B. Horner, Surgeon's Mate in the Revolutionary Army.

Gustuvus B. Horner, since deceased, who by his last **Will** and Testament, **probated on September 20, 1840** in Fauquier County, **bequeathed all that might come to him hereafter to be disposed of as James B. Thornton and wife Marianna should think proper for the benefit of their two children Alfred Thornton and Gustavus B. Thornton.**

Richard B. Horner, John S. Horner, Frederick Horner and Marianna Horner, the wife of James B. Thornton are the remaining heirs of Gustavus B. Horner. Marianna Horner Thornton leaves Alfred Horner, Gustavus B. James Thornton and Frances Mildred Thornton as her heirs at law.

Proof is now made with a view to obtaining a patent to the heirs of Dr. Gustavus B. Horner decd., to lands to which they are entitled from the United States for Horner's services as a Surgeon's Mate in the Revolutionary War.

These lands are to go to the heirs in the following proportions:
1/8th share to **Francis Whiting**
1/8th share to **Thomas L. Moore**, heir of Richard H. who was heir to his mother Elizabeth
1/8th share to **Catharine J. Marr**
1/8th share to **Richard B. Horner**
1/8th share to **John S. Horner**
1/8th share to **Frederick Horner**
1/8th share to **Alfred Horner, Gustavus B. James Thornton and Frances Mildred Thornton, children of Marianna Thornton decd.**
1/8th to **Alfred Thornton and Gustavus B. Thornton**, devisees of Gustavus B. Horner Jr.

<u>October 23, 1854 Court</u>   page 172.
It was this day proved to the satisfaction of the Court that **Susannah Drone decd., who was a pensioner of the United States at the rate of $100.00 per year, died on January 1, 1854, leaving John Drone, Nelly Drone, Richard Drone and Thomas Drone as her only children.**

Fauquier County Minute Book 1854-1855

October 23, 1854 Court   page 172. (Cont.)
Heirs at law of Susannah Drone, a Pensioner of the United States.

The administration of the estate of Susannah Drone decd., was granted to Robert E. Peyton, who gave bond and security according to law, the security having justified.

November 27, 1854 Court   page 188.
The Court ordered certified that upon the testimony of Richard Stone and T. B. Warder, two respectable citizens of this County, who are entitled to full confidence and have testified in open Court this day, after being duly sworn according to Law that **Jacob Preston decd., was a Revolutionary soldier. He died in 1804 and left a widow Cecilia Preston who died on December 9, 1847, still his widow. She never married again after Jacob Preston's death.**

Cecilia Preston had 12 children, the 1st, 3rd, 4th, 6th, 10th and 12th of whom have died. **There are now surviving:**
Allen Preston, the 2nd child, age 74.
Jane Kearns, the 5th child, age 69.
Agnes Sanford, the 7th child, age 67.
Jacob Preston, the 8th child, age 65.
Wm. Preston, the 9th child, age 63.
John Preston, the 11th child, age 57.
These are the 6 children of Cecelia Preston, now surviving.

It is ordered further certified that the affidavit of James Martin and Wm. Preston, taken before J. Willet Leach a Justice of the Peace for Fauquier County on October 25, 1854, and the certificates of J. Willet Leach thereto annexed were produced in open Court this day and the proceedings approved by the Court.

It is ordered further certified that Richard Stone and T. B. Warder further testify that they were personally acquainted with **John Preston of this County who subscribed and swore to his Declaration** on another page of this sheet, this day in open Court and in their presence, and knew him to be the same John Preston he **represented himself to be** in the Declaration – the **son of Cecilia Preston** with whom they were also personally acquainted.

Fauquier County Minute Book 1854-1855

February 27, 1855 Court   page 244.
On the motion of Bailey Carver, guardian **of Alice Jane Edmonds, the only minor child of Thornton Edmonds decd.** It appears to the satisfaction of the Court and is hereby certified by the County Court of Fauquier that **Thornton Edmonds, who was a Private in the Companies commanded by Captain Nimrod Ashby and Wm OBannon in the War of 1812 between the United States and Great Britain, died about November 5, 1854.**

The Court certifies that it appears to their satisfaction that the **wife of Thornton Edmonds eloped with another man some 15 years ago and has not been heard of since.**

The **laws of this State presume a person to be dead who has not been heard of for seven years** and the heir at law of Thornton Edmonds decd., Alice Jane Edmonds, is under 21 years of age.

On the motion of Bushrod P. Edwards, it appearing to the satisfaction of the Court, it is hereby certified by the Fauquier County Court, having probate jurisdiction, **that William Edwards, a Private in Captain James Payne's Company of Volunteer Riflemen in the War of 1812, died intestate on or about January 20, 1852.**

Bushrod P. Edwards, Wm. A. Edwards and Francis Weaver, the wife of Jacob P. Weaver, are the only children and heirs of Wm. Edwards, all of whom are over 21.

There are no debts against the estate of Wm. Edwards, the estate having been settled in 1854.

March 29, 1854 Court   page 268.
On the motion of L. F. W. Lake and it appearing to the satisfaction of the Court, it is hereby certified that **Isaac Lake, who served upwards of 14 days in the War of 1812 and was engaged in the Battle of the White House, died on March 26, 1851, leaving a widow Eleanor B. Lake. Eleanor B. Lake died on November 15, 1852.**

Arraminter D. Lake, Alvernon T. Lake, Isaac N. Lake, John L. Lake, Luther B. Lake and Thomas W. S. Lake are the only minor children and heirs at law of Isaac Lake decd.

Fauquier County Minute Book 1854-1855

<u>April 23, 1854 Court</u>   page 288.
On the motion of John T. Jeffries and it appearing to the satisfaction of the Court, it is hereby certified by the County Court of Fauquier, having full probate jurisdiction, that **Moses Jeffries, a private in Captain Digges' Volunteer Company in the 36th Regiment of Virginia Militia under General Hungerford in the War of 1812, died in the town of Warrenton around 1840.**
Mary Jeffries, the widow of Moses Jeffries, died in the latter part of 1852.
The only child of Moses and Mary Jeffries decd., under the age of 21, at this time is Sarah Ann Jeffries, aged about 19.
Mary Jeffries, in her life time, obtained a Land Warrant as the widow of Moses Jeffries for 40 acres under the Act of Congress passed September 20, 1850.

<u>Mary 29, 1855 Court</u>   page 305.
On the motion of Enoch M. Marshall, and it appearing to the satisfaction of the Court, it is hereby certified by the County Court of Fauquier, having full jurisdiction over the subject that **James Brown Marshall, late of this County, enlisted in Captain Cooper's Company, Colonel Child's Regiment in the Mexican War on or about October 23, 1847.**
James Brown Marshall died at Pueblo, Mexico on or about March 1848, unmarried and without issue.
James Brown Marshall's father died in 1842 and his mother died about October 1, 1854.
The only heirs at law of James Brown Marshall decd. are his brothers and sisters: Enoch M. Marshall, Mary A. Marshall, Wm. T. Marshall, Elmira T. Marshall, Margaret E. Marshall and Augusta Marshall. Augusta Marshall is an infant about 19 years old.

<u>June 26, 1855 Court</u>   page 350.
It is this day proved to the satisfaction of the Court that since the Certificate of this Court on December 23, 1854, the **following changes have occurred in reference to the heirs of Wm. Thayer, Revolutionary Soldier mentioned in the Certificate:**
Benjamin Felingame, is the husband of Betsey Thayer, daughter of Wm. Thayer. The name of the husband had been left blank in the Certificate made on December 23, 1854.

Fauquier County Minute Book 1854-1855

June 26, 1855 Court   page 350. (Cont.)
Heirs at law of Wm. Thayer, Revolutionary Soldier.

**Benjamin Felingame and Wm. Benjamin, husband of Sally
Thayer, another daughter of Wm. Thayer, have both died, leaving
their wives, Betsey (or Elizabeth) and Sally (or Sarah) surviving them
and who are still living.**
    **Taliaferro Thayer, a son of Wm. Thayer, has died unmarried and
intestate.**
    Upon the motion of Thomas S. Ashton, the same is ordered certified.

    On the motion of **Catherine F. Ball, sole infant child of Osburn
Ball decd. and Rosa Riley** and it appearing to the satisfaction of the
Court, it is hereby certified by the County Court of Fauquier **that Osburn
Ball, a Private in the War of 1812, who died three years ago** [in 1852],
had **first obtained a 40 acre Land Warrant under the Act of
September 1850.**
    **Osburn Ball cohabited with Rosa Riley,now living, for upwards
of 25 years before his death but was never lawfully married to her.
Osburn Ball and Rosa Riley lived together as man and wife, having a
large family of children, during the whole term of years as aforesaid.**
    **Catharine F. Ball was born during this cohabitation and was
recognized and reared as their child and is now nearly 20 years old
and the sole minor child of Osburn Ball decd.**
    By the laws of this State, she is an heir at law and entitled to all the
rights of descent and distribution relative to any estate, real an personal of
Osburn Ball decd. in as full and ample manner as if she had been born in
lawful wedlock.

August 25, 1855 Court   page 375.
    On the motion of James Blackwell, it is ordered to be certified to the
Secretary of the Department of Interior of the United States that the
following are **heirs of Joseph Blackwell decd., a Lieutenant and
Quartermaster in the Continental Line in the Revolutionary Army** to
whom scrip in lieu of a Bounty Land Warrant was issued by the State of
Virginia for military services.
    This decision, made by the United States Department of Interior, has
been ordered to be issued to his heirs for 4,000 acres of land.

Fauquier County Minute Book 1854-1855

<u>August 25, 1855 Court</u>   page 375. (Cont.)
**Heirs at law of Joseph Blackwell, a Lieutenant and Quartermaster in
the Continental Line in the Revolutionary War.**

Joseph Blackwell left surviving him sons John Blackwell, James
Blackwell, Wm. Blackwell and Joseph Blackwell. He left daughters
Ann Gaskins, wife of John H. Gaskins; Lucy Smith, wife of Wm. R.
Smith; and Agnes Jeffries, wife of Enoch Jeffries.

Joseph Blackwell and Wm. Blackwell both died intestate. Joseph
Blackwell left these surviving children: Octavia Chilton, wife of John
J. Chilton; Elizabeth Edmonds, wife of James H. Edmonds; Jane
Blackwell and James D. Blackwell.
Wm. Blackwell left these surviving children: James G. Blackwell,
Wm. Blackwell, Harriet E. Blackwell, Lucy H. Payne, wife of John D.
Payne; Sarah A. Keith, wife of Isham Keith Jr.; Ann E. Marshall, wife
of John Marshall; and Joseph Blackwell.

Ann E. Marshall and her husband have died intestate. Ann E.
Marshall left the following children: Ann Gordon Marshall, Margaret
L. Marshall, Fanny L. Marshall, John Marshall and Wm. C. Marshall,
all under age.

Joseph Blackwell, the son of Wm. Blackwell decd., died leaving 2
children: Joseph Blackwell and Ann Eliza Blackwell, both under age.

Agnes Jeffries has died intestate. Her husband is also dead.
Their surviving children are Joseph Jeffries, Enoch Jeffries, John
Jeffries, Eustace Jeffries, Lucy Jeffries and James Jeffries.

James Blackwell has died intestate, leaving a daughter
Josephine Blackwell, who is under age.

John H. Gaskins, the husband of Ann Gaskins, has died.

The **foregoing children, grandchildren and great grandchildren
of Joseph Blackwell decd. constitute his lawful heirs** and are the
present proprietors of the land scrip except the 1/3 thereof which has
been issued to Wm. Helm as assignee thereof.

Fauquier County Minute Book 1856-1857

September 23, 1856 Court   page 152.
It was proved to the satisfaction of the Court that **Mary Hixon was a Pensioner of the United States** at the rate of $125.00 per year. **She was a resident of Fauquier County and died here on July 16, 1846**, leaving one child only as her heir at law: **Amanda Klipstein.**

October 27, 1856 Court   pages 158-159.
The Court appoints **Thomas Birch, Captain; Levi Humner, Elijah Villett, Joseph Rice and John F. Thompson, a patrol for 3 months** in Magisterial District # 7.

The Court appoints **Ulysses Flemming, Captain; Andrew Cridler, James H. Reid, John T. Trunale, H. L. Johnson a patrol for 3 months** in District # 9.

December 22, 1856 Court   page 193.
On the motion of Enoch M. Marshall, Administrator of James Brown Marshall decd., the Court orders Isaac S. Tone, Meredith Eskridge, Stanton G. Embrey and Floda Humphreys, appointed Commissioners, any three of whom may act, to allot and **divide 1/7 slaves belonging to the estate of Mumford Marshall decd. as share of the estate of John Brown Marshall decd.**

The Court, not being fully advised of the necessity of appointing a general patrol for this County, decline making such appointment. Instead the Court recommend that the several Justices of the County appoint a patrol, as in their discretion, they may deem proper.
The Court orders that a copy of this order be furnished to the several Justices of the County.

March 23, 1857 Court   page 222.
On the motion of Augusta K. Marshall, and it appearing to the satisfaction of the Court, it is hereby certified by the County Court of Fauquier that **Augusta K. Marshall, youngest child of Mumford Marshall decd., to whom a Bounty Land Warrant (Duplicate) No. 75.200 for 120 acres has been issued because of the service of her deceased father Mumford Marshall in the War of 1812, attained her legal age of 21 on December 28, 1856.**

Fauquier County Minute Book 1856-1857

<u>March 27, 1857 Court</u>   page 237.
On the motion of Robert Utterback, the Court certifies that it was satisfactorily proved in open Court that **French Utterback, late of Fauquier County Virginia, died in Fauquier County in January 1857, intestate. He left no widow.**
His only heirs at law are his 4 children: Wm. Utterback, Robert Utterback, Margaret E. McClanahan, wife of David W. McClanahan; and Sarah Elizabeth Utterback, wife of Joseph N. Utterback.

<u>April 27, 1857 Court</u>   page 248.
On the motion of John W. Pattason and it appearing to the satisfaction of the Court, it is hereby certified by the County Court of Fauquier that **James S. Whiting, Thomas T. Whiting, Edward H. Whiting and Maria F. Patterson, wife of John W. Pattason are the only heirs of Washington J. Whiting who died in Alabama about two years ago** [in 1855].

The Court appoints **Enos Tate, Captain; Ambrose Cane and Thomas Tate a patrol** in Magisterial District # 1 of this County.

<u>September 28, 1857 Court</u>   pages 340-341.
On the motion of George W. Patten, and it appearing to the satisfaction of the Court, it is hereby certified that **James Lipscomb, a solider in the Revolutionary War, died ---- [left blank], leaving Foster B. Lipscomb and Marshall Lipscomb as his only heirs at law.**
Marshall Lipscomb is still living and Foster B. Lipscomb died in May 1854, leaving Harriett H. Lipscomb, now Harriet H. Patten, wife of George W. Patten and Moscow Lipscomb his only children and heirs at law. Moscow Lipscomb is under 21; Harriet H. Patten is over 21.
The Court further certifies that Robert Oliver and Samuel Weaver, whose names are signed to the bond hereto annexed, appeared in open Court this day and acknowledged their respective signatures thereto.
They are persons of respectability and character and fully responsible for the penalty stated in the bond. The bond is in due form and recoverable for the penalty therein stated agreeable to the laws of Virginia.

Fauquier County Minute Book 1856-1857

<u>September 28, 1857 Court</u>   pages 340-341.

Satisfactory evidence was exhibited to the Curt **that Judith Keith, a Pensioner of the United States** at the rate of $600.00 per year, an a resident of Fauquier County, **died on April 17, 1857. She left 4 children: Harriet Skinker, Mary J. Payne, Susan J. James and Isham Keith.**
John T. James is the Administrator duly authorized by this Court to act in that capacity on the estate of the deceased Pensioner.

<u>October 26, 1857 Court</u>   pages 349-350.
On the motion of L. F. W. Lake, and it appearing to the satisfaction of the Court, it is hereby certified by the County Court of Fauquier that **Isaac Lake, who served upwards of 14 days in the War of 1812 between the United States and Great Britain and was engaged in the Battle at the "White House" died on March 26, 1851. He left a widow, Eleanor B. Lake, who died in November 1852.**

Araminta D. Lake, Alvemon T. Lake, Isaac N. Lake, Thomas S. Lake, Luther B. Lake and Thomas W. S. Lake were the lawful and only minor children of their deceased father Isaac Lake at the date of their application for Bounty Land.

This application was made for the service of their deceased father Isaac Lake in the War of 1812 under the provision of the Act of congress passed March 5, 1855 and of others acts.

The father of the applicants was dead and no widow survived him at the date of their application for Bounty Land.

The applicants were the only lawful, surviving children of their deceased father and were all under legal age on March 3, 1855.

Their brother L. F. W. Lake qualified as their guardian in this Court, giving bond and security according to law.

As of May 28, 1855, the ages of the applicants were:
Araminta D. Lake, age 16, born February 12, 1839.
Alvernon T. Lake, age 20, born May 19, 1834.
Isaac N. Lake, age 17, born July 9, 1837.
John L. Lake, age 14, born October 19, 1840.
Luther B. Lake, age 12, born July 15, 1842.
Thomas W. S. Lake, age 9, born June 15, 1845.

Fauquier County Minute Book 1856-1857

<u>October 27, 1857 Court</u>   pages 349-350. (Cont.)
Heirs at law of Isaac Lake, a soldier in War of 1812.

The only lawful children of the deceased soldier, besides the minors, given above, are: L. F. W. Lake, Richard E. Lake, Thomas S. Lake, T. Marion Lake, Ludwell Lake, Harriet Fletcher, Emsey Glascock, Susan Lake and John W. Lake.

These children are all children by a former marriage of deceased soldier **Isaac Lake** and all are over 21 at the date of the application for bounty land or at the death of their father in 1851.

No other application has been made for the Bounty Land for services of Isaac Lake decd. than the one referred to.

Fauquier County Minute Book 1857-1859

<u>March 24, 1858 Court</u>   page 69.

It was proved to the satisfaction of the Court that **General Thomas Chilton decd. had two brothers and two sisters.**

One of General Chilton's brothers was **Joseph Chilton, who died leaving 6 children: Betsy Spilman, wife of Conway Spilman; Julia Keith, wife of Isham Keith; Joseph Chilton, Lucy Ann Johnston, wife of Edward P. Johnston; and John George Chilton. John George Chilton died in Kentucky and left a large family.**

His sister, **Nancy Chilton married Augustine Smith of Fauquier County and had the following children: Betsy Drew, wife of --- Drew, Thomas Smith, Charles C. Smith, John F. Smith (whose son is Charles E. Smith), Joseph Smith (now dead and leaving many children), Alexander H. Smith and Lucy C. Smith.**

<u>July 28, 1858 Court</u>   page 152.

It was proved to the satisfaction of the Court and ordered certified that **Benjamin Hellenius Bradford, the only son of Helen Bradford, and Colonel Benjamin R. Bradford, (both of whom are dead) died in Fauquier County Virginia** several years since, **unmarried and without issue.**

Fauquier County Minute Book 1857-1859

<u>July 28, 1858 Court</u>   page 152.
Heirs at law of Benjamin H. Bradford, only son of Colonel Benjamin R.
and Helen Bradford.

**Benjamin H. Bradford... died intestate and left as his heirs at law:
Alice T. Edmonds, wife of Alexander Edmonds; Margaret Edmonds,
widow of Sydner Edmonds, who reside in Fauquier County, Virginia;
and John Edmonds, who lives in Missouri. These heirs at laws are
his aunts and uncles.**

<u>November 23, 1858 Court</u>   page 213.
On the motion of Juliet Claggett, it appears to the satisfaction of the
Court from legal evidence introduced before this Court and is hereby
certified that **Elizabeth Cockerell, the half sister of Luther M. Sanford
decd., late of Fairfax County Virginia, died in 1855 or 1856.**

<u>December 27, 1858 Court</u>   page 246.
The Court appoints for two months from **today Peter Kemper, as
Captain and L. F. Ostrander, Andrew Jones, Norman Embrey and
Enoch M. Marshall, as patrols** of this County to act in the neighborhood
of Morrisville.

<u>January 24, 1859 Court</u>   page 256.
The Court certifies that **William Thayer, son of Wm. Thayer decd.,
who was a Sergeant Major in the Revolutionary War, having removed
from Virginia many years since to some of the western states** and
that, having not been heard from for more than 30 years, although diligent
enquiry has been made after him, **he has long been regarded by his
family as dead and would be presumed so by the law of Virginia**...
The Court is satisfied that Wm. Thayer is dead.

<u>January 24, 1859 Court</u>   page 256.
The Court orders it certified that it appears to this Court by satisfactory
evidence adduced in open Court that **Thomas Wiser died on March 22,
1856 in Fauquier County. Thomas Wiser died intestate, leaving
Elizabeth Wiser as his widow and the following children: 1) Henry T.
Wiser, 2) Mary Ann Wiser, 3) Charles T. Wiser, 4) John M. Wiser, 5)
Josiah Wiser.**

Fauquier County Minute Book 1857-1859

January 24, 1859 Court   page 256. (Cont.)
Heirs at law of Thomas Wiser, a soldier in the War of 1812.

These are the only and all heirs at law of Thomas Wiser at the time of his death. **His widow Elizabeth Wiser and his heirs above mentioned were issued Bounty Land Warrant No. 23441 for 80 acres for the services of Thomas Wiser in the War of 1812.** The widow and children are all adults and upwards of 21 as of September 1, 1858.

April 1, 1859 Court   page 296.
The Court certifies that it was established to its satisfaction today by competent and credible evidence adduced before it in open Court that **Captain James Wright of the Virginia Continental Line died intestate about 1812, leaving his daughter Elizabeth James, wife of John James, as his only heir at law.**

Elizabeth James died intestate, leaving her children David James, now living in Fauquier County Virginia; Aldridge James, Mary Smith, wife of Thompson Smith; and Margaret Kelly, wife of John P. Kelly as her only heirs at law.

Aldridge James, Mary Smith and Margaret Kelly have all died intestate.

The children and heirs at law of Aldridge James decd. are 1) Elizabeth Hord, wife of Dr. Ambrose Hord; 2) Edwin D. James, 3) Sarah E. James, 4) Susan K. James, 5) Waverly James, 6) Duncan James and 7) David James. All are adults and live in Fauquier County, Virginia.

The heirs at law and children of Mary Smith decd. are: 1) John Smith, 2) J. Aldridge Smith and 3) Augustin J. Smith, all of whom are adults.

The children and heirs at law of Margaret Kelly decd. at her death were: 1) Granville J. Kelly, 2) Jane Coleman, wife of Robert Coleman. Jane Coleman has died leaving children Granville Coleman and David Coleman. The third child of Margaret and John P. Kelly was Elizabeth Taliaferro, wife of Charles C. Taliaferro. She is also dead, leaving children John Taliaferro and Margaret Taliaferro.

Granville Coleman, David Coleman, John Taliaferro and Margaret Taliaferro are infants and Granville J. Kelly is their legal guardian.

Fauquier County Minute Book 1857-1859

<u>July 1, 1859 Court</u>   page 358.
The **Court order for April 1, 1858 touching the heirship of James Wright decd. is rescinded.**

Elizabeth James, daughter of Captain James Wright, died testate and by her will... made her son Aldridge James her sole residuary legatee after disposing of certain personal estate and land in Fauquier County.

Aldridge James died testate and devised his whole estate to his wife Elizabeth James. Elizabeth James, Aldridge's widow, died intestate.

The following people are her heirs at law: 1) **Elizabeth Hord, wife of Dr. Ambrose Hord; 2) Edwin D. James, 3) Sarah E. James, 4) Susan K. James, 5) Waverly James, 6) Duncan James, and 7) David James.**

All of the heirs at law of Elizabeth James are adults and reside in Fauquier County Virginia.

Fauquier County Minute Book 1859-1865

<u>April 24, 1860 Court</u>   page 128.
On the motion of E. N. Cologne, and it appearing to the satisfaction of the Court upon evidence this day offered in Court, it is hereby certified by the County Court of Fauquier County in the State of Virginia, having probat[e] jurisdiction, that **Garland B. Donaldson, a private in Captain Bell's Company of Virginia Militia in the War of 1812, died on or about December 12, 1855, unmarried and in[t]estate**, leaving his following **nephews and nieces as his heirs at law: Ann E. Lamarque, Mildred A. Michie, wife of John W. Michie; Mary Jane Graham, wife of David E. Graham; and Edgar N. Cologne.**

<u>August 30, 1860 Court</u> page 205.
It was this day proved to the satisfaction of the Court by evidence adduced before it that **Mary James was a United State Pensioner** at the rate of $42.00 per year and was a resident of Fauquier County, Virginia. **She died in Fauquier County March 23, 1860, leaving a grand child only whose name is Wm. H. Barbee and no other descendants.** Wm. H. Barbee is the administrator duly authorized by this Court to act in that capacity on the Estate of the deceased pensioner.

Fauquier County Minute Book 1859-1865

December 24, 1860   page 260.

The Court appoints **as the patrol of this County the Volunteer Company commanded by Captain Turner Ashby; the Black Horse Troop commanded by Captain John Scott; the Warrenton Riflemen commanded by John Q. Marr; and the Home Guard, commanded by Captain George W. Deatherage.**

The limits of Ashby's patrol shall be the Magisterial District of Farrowsville, Rectortown, The Plains and that portion of Salem above Carter's Run to the River.

The limits of Marr's and Deatherage's patrol shall be Warrenton and the adjacent County within 3 miles of the town.

The limits of Scott's patrol shall be the rest of the County.

The **officers commanding the patrols are ordered to use the utmost prudence and humanity in the discharge of their duties** and to allow no subordinate patrol to be detailed except under the command of some prudent and discreet Officer or private. **The officers are further directed to patrol only when and where necessary and the Justices of the County are requested to make no other appointments than the above.**

April 22, 1861 Court   page 317.

The Court hereby orders **bonds of this County** be issued for the sum of $20,000.00 in the aggregate, to be levied for at the next levy Court and payable as other portions of the County Levy which shall be **devoted to the equipment of the Volunteer Military Companies of this County.**

The bonds [are] to be signed by the Presiding Justice of this Court and to have the seal of the Court affixed thereto; and the Court hereby appoints John M. Forbes, Rice W. Payne and James V. Brooke a committee who shall superintend the appropriation of the funds and partition the same among the Volunteer Companies of this County now formed or hereafter to be formed according to their discretion.

The Committee [is] hereby empowered to sell the bonds upon the best terms they can procure and in such sums as they may in their discretion prescribe and to report their proceedings to the Court from month to month.

April 23, 1861 Court   page 319.

George W. Grayson resigned as Constable in District # 4. The Court directed a new election to be held at New Baltimore on the 4th Thursday in May next.

Fauquier County Minute Book 1859-1865

April 23, 1861 Court   page 319. (Cont.)
    N.M. Green resigned as Constable in District # 7. The Court
directed a new election to be held at Salem and Orlean on the 4th
Thursday in May next.

May 27, 1861 Court   pages 322-323.
    The Court appoints the **Lee Guard and the Home Guard a patrol for
the town of Warrenton and immediate neighborhood.**
    The Court appoints as **Special Police** for this County the following
persons, to wit – **H. A. White, Captain; J. V. Brooke, Thomas E.
Saunders, Robert C. Newby, Wm. H. Gaines, Alfred Gaskins and Jon
A. Chilton.**

June 24, 1861 Court   page 328.
    From the County Levy:
        To amount for equipment of Volunteers,} $20,000.00
        Military Companies of County}

June 24, 1861 Court   page 332.
    The Court authorizes the Military committee of this County **to transfer
to the members of Wm. N. Thorn's Guerilla Company any uniform**
which may be **returned to them by members of Captain Wigfield's
Company.**

June 27, 1861 Court   page 331.
    A **vacancy occurred in District # 5** of the County **in the number of
Justices of the Peace** which the **County** is **authorized** by law **to elect,
occasioned by the death of John Q. Marr.** The Court orders a writ of
Election to supply the vacancy be issued by the Clerk of Court, directed to
Cyrus Cross, commanding him to hold the election according to law in the
town of Warrenton on July 13, 1861...

June 27, 1861 Court   page 334.
    The Court orders **Henry Green**, a suspicious character committed to
the Jail of this County by a Justice of the Peace thereof, be sent to
General Beauregard to be dealt with as he thinks proper.

Fauquier County Minute Book 1859-1865

<u>July 23, 1861 Court</u>   page 335.

It is ordered that the Clerk of the Court enroll **male free Negroes of this County between the ages of 18-50** in pursuance of an ordinance of the Convention of the State of Virginia entitled an ordinance to provide for the enrollment and employment of free Negroes in public services passed July 1, 1861 – and return the enrollment to his office.

<u>July 26, 1861 Court</u>   page 339.

It was this day proved to the satisfaction of the Court that **Joseph B. Lunsford, son of Wormley Lunsford** of Fauquier County **and a member of Captain Edmond Berkeley's Company of Virginia Volunteers was killed at the Battle of Manassas on July 26, 1861** and that Joseph B. Lunsford **at the time of his death was under 21.**

<u>September 23, 1861 Court</u>   page 343.

On the Petition of **C.K. Marshall of Mississippi, acting as assistant Quartermaster of the Army of Mississippi** and [as] general agent of Military associations of the State of Mississippi for the relief of Volunteers, **it is ordered by the Court that the basement room of the Courthouse may be used as a Hospital for the sick and wounded Mississippians or others who may be ordered to this post.**

<u>October 30, 1861 Court</u>   page 346.

A certificate of qualification of **John A. Washington** to his **commission as Lieutenant Colonel** was returned to the Court and ordered recorded.

<u>October 30, 1861 Court</u>   page 347.

A paper purporting to be **the last Will and Testament of John A. Washington decd. was produced to the Court...** The Court ordered it to be recorded.

<u>March 24, 1862 Court</u>   page 374.

On the motion of **Wm. A. Jennings, Clerk of Fauquier County Court, to consider the propriety of removing the records of the Court to a place of safety in consequence of an invasion of the County by the Public Enemy. On consideration whereof and for reasons appearing to the Court, it is ordered that the records remain on file in the Clerk's Office of the Court.**

Fauquier County Minute Book 1859-1865

<u>July 25, 1864 Court</u>   page 389.
    It is ordered that the several Justices of the County be summoned to appear here on the 1st of September Term 1864 of this Court to consider **the propriety of appointing an agent or agents for this County with the power of impressment under the Act of the General Assembly of Virginia passed October 31, 1863 and style an Act for the relief of the Indigent Soldiers and Sailors of the State of Virginia** who have been or may be disabled in the Military Service, and the widows and minor children of Soldiers and Sailors who have died or may hereafter die in service, and of the indigent families of those now in service.

<u>September 26, 1864 Court</u>   page 392.
    The **Court appoints Sampson P. Bayly, agent for Fauquier County** under an Act of the General Assembly of Virginia passed October 31, 1863 and styled "An Act for Relief of Indigent Soldiers and Sailors of the State of Virginia who have be4en or may be disabled in the Military Service, and the widow and minor children of Soldiers and Sailors who have died or may hereafter die in said Service and of the Indigent families of those now in service" and **does authorize him to purchase for the use and support of such person** (for 6 months from October 1, 1864) **300 barrels of flour and 300 barrels of corn** at prices not exceeding those prescribed by Commissioners appointed for the State of Virginia under an Act of Congress of Confederate States regulating impressments.
    The Court orders the Sheriff of Fauquier County to summon the several justices thereof to appear here on the first day of the next term of the Court to consider the propriety of giving the agent the power of impressing the supplies.

    Ordered that the **Sheriff of this County do make a list of all indigent soldier and sailor, enlisted from the County in the Confederate service or State service who have been or may be disabled or honorably discharged and of the widows and minor children of such as may have died or may hereafter die in the service and return the same to the Clerk's office of this Court by the next term of this Court.**
    It is **also requested that the Magistrates in each magisterial district report a list of these persons** and their families in their respective districts to the next term of this Court.

Fauquier County Minute Book 1859-1865

November 28, 1864 Court   pages 395-396.
On the motion of Samuel W. Skinker, it is ordered **that Anderson D. Smith, "Cotton and Salt Agent for Fauquier County"** be summoned to appear here on the first day of the next term of this Court to shew cause, if any he can, why his powers and authorities as an agent shall not be annulled and revoked.

The Court orders that **Anderson D. Smith, Salt Agent for this County,** be and he is hereby required to take a receipt from each individual or his agent to whom he shall deliver County salt, specifying the number of lbs. delivered each, and shall keep a column in his account setting for the same, also that he present a full list of the numbers of persons to whom he has heretofore delivered salt, the quantity to each and the amount of money paid by each.

On the motion of **Sampson P. Bayly, agent for Fauquier County** under the act of the General Assembly of Virginia passed October 31, 1863 and style "An act for the relief of Indigent Soldiers +c"
It is ordered that he be, and he is hereby, empowered to impress the amount of supplies which he has heretofore been authorized to purchase by an order of the Court of September 26, 1864, the agent substituting an equivalent amount of wheat in place of flour whenever he deems it necessary.
Whereupon Sampson P. Bayly gave bond as such with security according to law, the security having justified. The Agent is required to report his proceedings to the Court.

The Court hereby orders that bonds of the County be issued for the sum of $10,000.00 in the aggregate. The **bonds** [are] to be signed by the Presiding Justice of this Court and to have the seal of the Court affixed thereto, to be levied upon the County and payable in 20 years from this date, which shall be **devoted to the purchase of supplies for the relief of Indigent Soldier +c** under an Act of the General Assembly of Virginia passed October 31, 1863 and styled "An act for the Relief of Indigent Soldiers +c." and shall be sold for cash to the highest bidder at public auction in the town of Warrenton.

The County Court of this County learns with much surprise and regret that an Assessor and Collector of Taxes under the Act of the Confederate Congress passed the --- day of --- 186- has been appointed for this County and are ordered to enter upon the discharge of their duties.

Military Records, Pension Applications and Heirs at Law of Soldiers
from Fauquier County, Virginia Court Minute Books Volume 3 1840-1904

46

Fauquier County Minute Book 1859-1865

<u>November 28, 1864 Court</u>   pages 395-396. (Cont.)

[We] take occasion respectfully to draw the attention of the proper authorities and of the Congress of the Confederate States to the **peculiarly unfortunate situation in which the people of this County have been left in consequent of the invasion and occupation of it by the Public Enemy since the withdrawal of the Confederate forces from Manassas Junction.**

The extent to which the property of the people has been despoiled can only be approximated by an inspection of the face of the Country and where the devastated homesteads, the burn mansions, fields once blooming with crops and alive with lowing herds now wasted with violence, the woodland stripped of their trees present an inadequate idea of the consequences to the proprietors of the real damage done them.

All these ill effects, great and grievous as they are, together with the loss of labor, have been borne unmumuringly by our citizens and they remain as loyal to the Confederate government and the cause of the South as the people of any portion of the Confederate States.

But now while the gross products of the County are barely, if indeed they be sufficient for the substance of its population to have the tax collector to draw their last shilling, to be raised by the sale of their capital is [word illegible]; they but little expected and against which they most earnestly protest and feel sadly aggrieved.

They therefore pray that they be relieved from this additional burthen and that the appointment of the officers aforesaid be revoked and all efforts to collect taxes of our people be abandoned.

<u>January 23, 1865</u>   page 397.
Whereas **General Wm. H. Payne, Commonwealth Attorney for this County is now and necessarily absent from the County with his command in the field during the war, and it is deemed essential that the Commonwealth should be represented by counsel**, therefore it is ordered that **J. M. Spilman and he is hereby requested to act** in the place of General Payne as **Commonwealth Attorney** during his absence in the field as aforesaid.

Fauquier County Minute Book 1859-1865

<u>January 23, 1865 Court</u>   page 397.
    It is ordered that **Wm. M. Hume, Sheriff of Fauquier County, sell the County bonds** (ordered to be issued at the November term 1864 of this Court) for $10,000.00 in the aggregate at the next term of this Court and that the bonds be issued as follows: $2000.00 in $100.00 bonds each and the residue $8,000.00 in $500.00 bond each.

<u>January 27, 1865 Court</u>   page 398.
    On the motion of Wm. A. Jennings, Clerk of Fauquier County Court, it is ordered that the **Court be held in the Clerk's Office thereof until further orders in consequence of the ill conditions of the Courthouse of the Court, occasioned by the Public Enemy.**

    On the motion of Richards Payne, the Court orders the sale of County bonds advertised to be sold today for the relief of Indigent soldiers +c. be and the same is hereby postponed until further orders. ꞌ
    That the bonds bear interest at the rate of 6% per year, payable annually from the date thereof.
    That [the Court] fix the price of corn at $6.00 per barrel and of wheat, at $2.00 per bushel.
    That [the Court] further order Sampson P. Bayly (Impressment agent of Fauquier County) to offer to all persons from whom he may have or shall hereafter procure supplies, the option of taking such bonds in payments thereof at the above prices. The agent is to report his proceedings to the Court at its next term.

Fauquier County Minute Book 1865-1867

<u>April 24, 1865 Court</u>   page 1.
    Ordered that **A.D. Smith, Salt Agent for the County, sell the salt** belonging to the County **now on hand for Gold or its equivalent** at such time and manner he may think best.

Fauquier County Minute Book 1865-1867

<u>August 28, 1865 Court</u> pages 6-7.
Letter from William H. Payne

Warrenton. August 28, 1865
To the Worshipful Justices of the County Court of Fauquier County
    I am informed that in the Election ordered by the Governor in July last, the people of this County by an overwhelming vote expressed their desire that I should continue as the Commonwealth Attorney of this County.
    Not knowing then of any obstacle to my qualifying, and indeed ignorant <u>now</u> of any <u>legal</u> difficulty, I confidently relied upon enjoying this mark of the confidence and kindness of my people.
    I am informed however that a different construction of Constitution and law prevails in others quarters and that an attempt to avail myself of this expression in my favor would put the people of the County in a false position and probably impede their reorganization.
In fact I am informed that you have been ordered by the Governor to reject any Confederate officer who may have been elected to Office. The dilemma is thus presented of submission to these orders, extraordinary as they are, or a decision of this Court which will bring it into contact with the powers of the State. The times do not leave me a choice. I am too eager for restoration of order myself, and too grateful to my country man [men?] for their lately offered kindness to bring further affliction or distrust upon them.
    I therefore return the office of Commonwealth Attorney to them declaring at the same time that I believe myself eligible to the office, and that I am supported in that opinion by the attestation of our Judges. And as far as I can have a large majority of the Bar of the State, declaring further that at this particular moment, there is no legal power in any quarters to contest my eligibility and that I therefore voluntarily surrender the Office to promote the harmony and peace of the community and to aid in the establishment of the government. The Court can now seek some one more acceptable to the authorities upon whom to confer the office.
    Respectfully your Ob. ser^{t}
                         (signed) William H. Payne.

<u>August 28, 1865 Court</u> page 7.

Richard H. Carter, who was duly elected as Justice of the Peace in District # 9... this day **declined to qualify... and offered to the Court the following paper...**

Fauquier County Minute Book 1865-1867

<u>August 28, 1865 Court</u>   page 7.
Letter from Richard H. Carter (Cont.)

Glen Welby Fauquier County, Virginia, August 28, 1865
To the Worshipful County Court of Fauquier
Gentlemen:
    I have received information that at the Election recently held under Executive Order for County Officers I was re-elected a member of your body and subsequently I have learned that, in consequence of having held a military commission in the Confederate service, it has been decided I was not eligible to the position, cheerfully acquiescing in that decision.
    I hereby, Gentlemen, respectfully decline offering to qualify to my commission, believing prior to the Election that I was eligible I signified my willingness to serve if the people of my district thought proper to elect me. I regret that the mistake under which the voters of the district as well as myself labored should have caused the necessity for another Election.
    With the foregoing remarks, Gentlemen, I might be content. But in view of my long connection with your body, and the probable fact, that the connexion is now permanently dissolved – you will, I trust, indulge me in a few words personal to myself, and not, I think, inappropriate to the occasion.
    In 1837 or 1838, and before I had attained the legal age, I was nominated and in due time thereafter commissioned a Justice of the County. Ever since which time I have retained the Office until I am now perhaps older in Commission than any other Justice of the County.
    I was proud of the honor and trust thus bestowed upon me, and in entering upon my duties felt determined to discharge them faithfully, honestly and to the full measure of my ability, and now, Gentlemen, I fee assured I have fully discharged my trust. whether upon the Bench or in the discharge of the neighborhood business.
    I have endeavored to be faithful and impartial. I have sought no other approval than that of my own conscience and judgment. My intercourse with the individual members of your body has been uniformly of the most agreeable kind. My relations with all have been friendly and kind, having the fullest confidence in your integrity and hoping that your organization will speedily restore to our people all the benefits of our laws. I will conclude with assurances of the high regard and esteem of
        Respectfully y^r Ob. S^t,
               (signed) Richard H. Carter

Fauquier County Minute Book 1865-1867

<u>August 28, 1865 Court</u>   page 8.
Ordered that **John M. Forbes, J. Blackwell Smith and John G. Beckham... are appointed Commissioners of Public Buildings** for this County. The Commissioners are hereby directed to contract forthwith for necessary repairs to the County Jail. It is further ordered that the Commissioners advertise for proposals for such repairs as in their judgment may be necessary to the Court house and Clerk's Offices of this County and make report as to these buildings to the Court.

<u>August 29, 1865 Court</u>   pages 9-10.
A vacancy occurred in the Office of Commonwealth Attorney by reason of the **ineligibility of William H. Payne**. The Court directed a new Election to be held by the Sheriff...

Vacancies occurred in the Offices of Justice of the Peace in District 5 and District 9 by reason of the **ineligibility of John Ward [District 5] and Richard H. Carter [District 9]; also in District 5 in the Office of Overseer of the Poor, by reason of the ineligibility of Edwin Smith**. The Court orders elections to be held by the Sheriff...

<u>August 30, 1865 Court</u>   page 13.
The Court appoints **Horace Pattie as superintendent of the Court house** and orders the sum of $80.00 annually be levied for him for his services.

John S. Mosby, who has been duly licensed in this state to practice law, having this day taken the several oaths prescribed by law, and having subscribed the oath prescribed by the first section of an Act of the general Assembly of Virginia entitled "An Act to Amend and re-enact the Act prescrib8ing Oaths in certain cases and providing for the registration of the same," passed May 14, 1862, **leave is granted him to practice law in this Court.**

<u>September 25, 1865 Court</u>   pages 23-24.
Memorial of the County Court of Fauquier to the Legislature of Virginia.
The County Court of Fauquier County respectfully states to the Hon: Legislature of Virginia that the Courthouse, Jail and Courtyard, of their County, have been very materially injured by their occupation by troops, almost continually from the commencement of the War, and that it will require a large sum of money to place them in a proper state of repair.

Fauquier County Minute Book 1865-1867

September 25, 1865 Court   pages 24-25 (Cont.)
Memorial from Justices of the County to the Virginia Legislature
(Cont.)

That even if this Court had power under existing laws to lay a levy at any term prior to that of May or June next, yet a levy so laid would be productive of much injury, and operate unequally upon the people of the County from the fact that it could now be laid solely on landed property, for there are but few products in the hands of our people by a sale of which money can be raised, their maintenance for the year being a task with difficulty accomplished amid the dilapidation, ruin and loss of labor incident to our situation;

They also state that the poor of the County have to be provided for during the ensuing winter, and that there are not funds in the hands of the authorities of the County, and they have exhausted their credit, nor can any list of the tithables or poll tax payers be placed in the hands of the Sheriff, the Commissioners of Revenue not having been able in consequence of the presence of the Federal Army, to attend to this or any other duty since 1861.

The only recourse left is to raise the necessary funds by procuring a loan and pledging the County for its payment in the future – as a requisite to the success of this scheme, the authority of your honorable body must be obtained.

Your memorialists therefore respectfully ask the enactment of a law of the tenor and effect of that accompanying this petition.

1st. be it enabled by the General Assembly of Virginia that the County Court of Fauquier County be and is hereby authorized and empowered at any term thereof to issue bonds in the name of the County of Fauquier, for such sum or sums of money as the Justices composing the Court may in their discretion determine, not exceeding in the aggregate the sum of $5,000.00 and to sell the bonds, and with the proceeds of sales, to repair and improve, in such manner as the Court may think proper, the Courthouse, Jail and Public Lot of the County, and appropriate so much of the proceeds as the Court may deem necessary, to the support and maintenance of the poor of the County.

2nd. That the bonds issued in pursuance of this act shall be made payable within not less than two nor more than five years from the date thereof, shall be signed by the presiding Justice of the County Court, be attested by the Clerk thereof, and have the seal of the Court affixed thereto.

Fauquier County Minute Book 1865-1867

<u>September 25, 1865 Court</u> page 25 (Cont.)
Memorial from the Justices of the County to the Virginia Legislature
(Cont.)

3rd. That the debts contracted and evidenced by the bonds shall be levied for by the County Court of the County, upon such subjects of taxation as are or may be liable by law for the County Levy, and that the faith of the County is pledged for the punctual payment of the principal and interest of the bonds, when the same shall come due.

4th. This act shall be in force from its passage.

<u>September 25, 1865 Court</u> page 25
   Vacancies having occurred in the Offices of Constable in District # 1 and 4 by reason of the **ineligibility of O.P. Embry and the failure of George W. Grayson to qualify.**
   Also in District # 1 in the Office of Justice of the Peace, by reason of **removal [from office] of John L. Crittenden.** The Court orders a new election to be held by the Sheriff.

<u>October 23, 1865 Court</u>   page 35.
   Vacancies have occurred in the Offices of Overseers of the Poor in District # 3 and for Constable in District # 4 due to **the ineligibility of R. H. Downman** [for District # 3] and the **failure of George W. Grayson** [District # 4] **to qualify.** The Court directs elections to be held by the Sheriff...

The Court ordered the following **memorial to the Honorable Andrew Johnson, President of the United States**... and appoints the Honorable W.W. Payne to deliver an authenticated copy of the Memorial to his Excellency.

To His Excellency, **Andrew Johnson, President of the United States**
   The County Court of Fauquier, State of Virginia, beg leave to represent
   • that four years of War have so impoverished the people of this County that much suffering for the necessaries of life has occurred, and that much more must occur the coming winter.

Fauquier County Minute Book 1865-1867

<u>October 23, 1865 Court</u>   page 35.
Memorial to Andrew Jackson, President of the United States
(Cont.)

•   that the Crops of 1862, 1863 and 1864 were generally used or destroyed by passing armies, that the Crop of the present year are very inadequate to the wants of the people, that the livestock has nearly disappeared, and that there is no prospect for amelioration in the condition of the people before the end of next year.

•   In the midst of such destitution, with many dwelling homes and farm buildings destroyed or in ruins, with more than half the arable land of the County turned into common for want of fences, and no adequate force of horses, oxen and labor to cultivate the enclosed land, the tax gatherer has appeared among us, demanding under the laws of the United States Congress of August 5, 1861 and July 7, 1862, twenty-seven cents upon each $100.00 of land of the valuation of 1860 – which aggregate amounts to a very large sum of money, greatly more than is believed to be possessed by the entir3e population of the County.

•   Should the collection be persisted in, connected with other burdens, it will lead to great sacrifices in raising money with some, while to others, it will amount to a forfeiture of their lands, by a sale for taxes, and render all in subsequent years less able to withstand the taxation necessary to support the credit of the government.

•   Under the circumstances, we beg leave to ask that the collection of the land tax may be suspended for the present, or at least so modified as to some proportion to the present value of the respective tracts of land, there being a wide difference between the value of them in 1860 and their value now, and between a farm wasted by war and a farm left in the condition it was when assessed.

<u>December 25, 1865 Court</u>   page 78.
    The General Assembly of Virginia by their act passed December 14, 1865, having authorized the County Court of this County to borrow upon the credit of the County a sum of money, not exceeding $5,000.00;

Fauquier County Minute Book 1865-1867

<u>December 25, 1865 Court</u>   page 78.
It is ordered that the several Justices of the County by summoned to attend here on the first day of next January term of this Court to consider and determine [what] the Court shall do under this act.

<u>December 25, 1865 Court</u>   pages 81-83.
The Court passed resolutions regarding **the deaths of 1) Judge John Webb Tyler**, Judge 9th Judicial Circuit of Virginia; 2) **Robert E. Scott in May 1862**; 3) Attorneys **Robert Randolph, J.W. Kincheloe and Madison Tyler** as part of the Military; 4) **B. Tebbs and P. Bell Smith; 5) Captain John Q. Marr.**

<u>January 22, 1866 Court</u>   pages 93-94.
The Justices of the County ordered that $5,000.00 worth of bonds of Fauquier County, in pursuance of the provision of an Act of Assembly, be issued in sums of not less than $100.00 each, to bring interest at the rate of 6% per year for their respective dates. The bonds are to be made payable as follows:

- $1,500.00 to be payable January 1, 1869, interest paid January 1 of each year.
- $1,500.00 to be payable January 1, 1870, interest paid January 1 of each year.
- $2,000.00 to be payable January 1, 1871, interest paid January 1 of each year.

The Court orders none of the bonds sold at a greater rate of discount than 10%. The Court ordered the proceeds from the sale of the bonds to be applied 1) to repairs of the Jail, Court house and other Public property on the public square in the town of Warrenton and to the support and maintenance of the Poor of the County since April 1, 1865. 2) the residue is to be applied to the payment of necessary debts contracted by the Count for the support and maintenance of the Poor thereof prior to April 1, 1865, provided that this class of County creditors shall consent to take in discharge of their several claims the bonds at their par value.

It is ordered that all the creditors of the County for or on account of support and maintenance of the Poor do fill all such claims before the aforesaid Commissioners who are hereby directed to audit the same. All such claims dated prior to April 1, 1865 are to be made upon a specie basis at the time said claims respectively accrued.

Fauquier County Minute Book 1865-1867

January 22, 1866 Court   pages 93-94.
It is ordered that all bonds authorized by this order shall be printed, signed by the presiding Justice of the Court, attested by the Clerk thereof and have the seal of the Court affixed.
On the foregoing several propositions, Justices voted viva voce. Voting yes:
Samuel T. Ashby, R. H. Francis, Thomas Henderson, A.D. Priest, Joseph W. Colbert, J. B. Cummins, John G. Beckham, R. T. Mitchell, Wm. J. Morgan, S. W. Skinker, John R. Hart, C. H. Tavenner, Joseph B. Smith, Robert Hume, James Priest, Jas. S. Thornton, William H. Gaines.

Voting No:
John M. Fant, S. H. Newhouse, Stanton G. Embrey, Lewis Shumate, N. H. Crump, Isaac S. Stone, B.T. Rixey

January 22, 1866 Court   page 95.
Anderson D. Smith, heretofore appointed salt agent for this County, this day made his report to the Court. On consideration of which the Court accepts and confirms the report and return to him their thanks for the manner in which he has discharged the duties of his agency.

June 25, 1866 Court   page 199.
Anderson D. Smith, late Salt agent for this County, having paid to **Wm. H. Gaines, Presiding Justice of this Court** the sum of $300.00 on account of salt in his hands at the surrender of the Confederate forces, the Court orders this sum paid by Wm. H. Gaines into the hands of the Commissioners of Public Buildings, who are instructed to purchase rope carpeting and cover the Court room with the same. If any funds remain after the purchase [of the rope carpeting], the Commissioners are instructed to expand such remainder into a chair for the Court room.

July 23, 1866 Court   pages 209-210.
The **Report of Commissioners Gains, Forbes and Bryne** under the order of the Court dated January 22, 1866, **of their action in regard to the sale of County bonds and the unsettled account against the County for the support of the Poor prior to April 1, 1865 was this day returned to Court.**

Fauquier County Minute Book 1865-1867

July 23, 1866 Court   pages 209-210.
    B F Rixey and Richard A. Thompson appeared by their counsel and
opposed the confirmation of the report so far as it relates to them, on the
grounds of the insufficiency of their several allowances. The parties were
fully heard and the Court overruled all objections to the report and
approved and confirmed the same.

    The Court ordered each and all creditors of the County, mention in the
report, whose claims exceed $100.00, receive from the Commissioners
the County bonds for the hundred or hundreds in discharge thereof.
Fractions of their claims being less than $100.00 shall be levied for at the
present term of the Court.

    A report of the Commissioners of Public Buildings was this day
returned to the Court. There being no exception or objection thereto, the
same was confirmed.

July 25, 1866 Court   page 223.
    Company 7 of the 85th Regiment of Virginia Militia, having failed to
elect proper officers, the Court recommends the following persons to the
Governor as suitable officers: **James D. Kirby, as Captain; Gustavus B.
Horner, as 1st Lieutenant and Thomas William Tongue as 2nd
Lieutenant.**

May 27, 1867 Court   page 374.
    The Court certifies that **William H. Triplett** and **Jeremiah Heflin** are
residents of Virginia and that **they lost arms in the late war.**

Fauquier County Minute Book 1867-1869

July 22, 1867 Court   page 9
    The Court certifies that **George W. Davis** is a resident of the State of
Virginia and that **he lost a leg in the late war.**

August 26, 1867 Court   page 22.
    Benjamin F. Rixey, having produced before the Court satisfactory
evidence that certain bonds executed by Fauquier Count, by authority of
an Act of the General Assembly of Virginia passed December 14, 1863
and transferred and delivered to Rixey for value. **These bonds have
been lost or stolen from him.**

Fauquier County Minute Book 1867-1869

<u>August 26, 1867 Court</u> page 22 (Cont.)
These bonds (which were either lost or stolen) were delivered to Benjamin
F. Rixey:
- 3 bonds (#s 22, 23, and 24) each for $100.00 dated July 23, 1866,
payable January 1, 1869
- 5 bonds (#s 25, 26, 27, 28 and 29), each for $100.00, also dated
July 23, 1866, and payable January 1, 1870.

The interest on these bonds has been paid to January 1, 1867.
Having further proved that notice of his loss has been duly published for 4
weeks in the "True Index"... without effect, the Court orders **Wm. H.
Gaines, John M. Forbes and John S. Byrne**, Commissioners appointed
by this Court under its order January 22, 1866 to issue to Rixey duplicates
of the lost bonds, corresponding to the description above, which shall be
in lieu of the bonds so lost or stolen.

<u>October 28, 1867 Court</u> pages 57-58.
    On the motion of L. L. Lomax, it was proved to the satisfaction of the
Court that **Elizabeth V. Lomax was a Pensioner of the United States** at
the rate of $30.00 per month; that she was a **resident of Fauquier
County, Virginia; that she died May 7, 1867; that she left four
daughters – Virginia, Victoria, Julia and Mary Lomax,** all of whom are
21 years old and unmarried.

<u>August 27, 1868 Court</u> page 227.
    Nimrod Marks v. Isaac L. N. Hazen – On a Judgment of Fauquier
County Court rendered at its May Court 1867.
    In obedience to military orders and instructions herewith filed, the
proceedings in this cause are reversed and annulled, and in further
obedience to the orders, it is considered by the Court that the defendant J.
L. N. Hazen recover against Nimrod Marks, the sum of $80.13, being the
entire costs which Hazen has had to pay, or is liable to pay, in the
proceedings in this cause, as appears from the records of this Court.
[Margin Note: "Filed in papers of May Court 1867.]

<u>April 26, 1869 Court</u> page 303.
    **James M. Catlett, H. P. Wait, H. H. Robertson, Cumins Buchanan
and J. H. Evans produced to the Court evidence of their
appointments as Justices of Peace for this County, by the Military
Commander of the first Military District, State of Virginia,** and of their
qualification as such, which is ordered to be filed among the records of
this Court.

Fauquier County Minute Book 1867-1869

<u>April 26, 1869 Court</u>   page 303 (Cont.)
   James Rogers this day produced to the Court evidence of his
qualification as Clerk of the Court, which is ordered to be entered of
record, and is in the words and figures following, to wit:
In the Circuit Court of Fauquier County 6th of April 1869
   James Rogers produced to the Court **evidence of his appointment**
by **George Stoneman, Brevet Major General, United States Army,
commanding the first Military District, State of Virginia,** as Clerk of
**the County Court of Fauquier Count, in the place of William A.
Jennings, removed,** and **James Rogers, together with T. N. Fletcher,
John A. Spilman, John H. Rixey and William J. Morgan, as his
securities,** who justified as to their sufficiency, thereupon entered into
and acknowledged in open Court, a bond, payable and conditioned as the
law directs, in the penalty of $10,000.
   James Rogers also took and subscribed in open Court the oath
prescribed by the Act of Congress of July 2, 1862, the oath of Fidelity to
the Commonwealth of Virginia, the oath to support the Constitution of the
United States, the anti-dwelling oath and the oath of office. The bond is
ordered to be recorded as the law directs.
   A copy teste, **R. L. Reilly, Clerk.**

<u>April 26, 1869 Court</u>   page 307.
   On the motion of **F.M. Fletcher, Commissioner of Revenue for this
County in District # 2, who represents he is unable to perform his
duties** as such Commissioner, The **Court appoints Silas H. Turner to
assist him in the discharge of his duties.**
   Thereupon S. H. Turner took the oath of Fidelity to the
Commonwealth, oath to support the Constitution of the United States, the
anti-dwelling oath and the oath of office.

   On the motion of **A.J. Parr, Commissioner of Revenue for this
County in District # 1, who alleges he is unable to perform his duties**
as such Commissioner, the **Court appoints Nimrod Ashby to assist
him in the discharge of his duties.**
   Thereupon Nimrod T. Ashby took the oath of Fidelity to the
Commonwealth of Virginia, the oath to support the Constitution of the
United States, the anti-dwelling oath, and the oath of office.

Fauquier County Minute Book 1867-1869

<u>April 26, 1869 Court</u>   page 308.
The Court recommends to the General commanding the first Military District, State of Virginia, the appointment of **E.T. Holton as Justice of Peace in the 7th Magisterial District of this County**, the Court being satisfied that he is a loyal and competent man and will qualify if appointed.

L L Lewis produced to the Court evidence of his appointment as Commonwealth Attorney for this County by George Stoneman, the General commanding the first Military District, State of Virginia, in place of E.M. Spilman, removed.

Whereupon L.L. Lewis in open Court qualified as such by taking the oath prescribed by the Act of July 2, 1862., the oath to support the Constitution of the United States, the oath of Fidelity to the Commonwealth of Virginia, the anti-dwelling oath and the oath of office.

L L Lewis produced to the Court evidence of his being licensed to practice as an Attorney at Law in the Courts of the Commonwealth and in open Court took the oath required of attorneys and the oath of Fidelity to the Commonwealth of Virginia, whereupon he is admitted to practice as an attorney at law in this Court.

<u>April 27, 1869 Court</u>   page 312.
William H. Gaines, in whose hands $1,800.00 was levied at the last June term of this Court, to pay the County bonds which would mature on January 1, 1869, and the interest in other outstanding County bonds falling due on that date, this day returned to the Court a report of his action in the matter, together with the County bonds to the amount of $1,500.00 which he has paid off and taken in.

Whereupon the Court orders... the report and bonds to be filed among the records of this Court.

<u>April 27, 1869 Court</u>   pages 313-314.
The Justices constituting this Court, being, all with one exception, appointed by the Military Commander of this District, deeming it better to postpone until the next term of this Court the choice of a Presiding Justice, by which time other Justices will probably have been appointed.

Fauquier County Minute Book 1867-1869

<u>April 27, 1869 Court</u>   pages 313-314 (Cont.)
But [the Justices], deeming it necessary that there should be a Presiding Justice in the interval between this and the next term of this Court, in order that records for other states may be properly authenticated under the laws of Congress, by a unanimous vote elected H. H. Robertson to be Presiding Justice to hold his office until the next term of this Court. and no longer unless again elected... (signed) **H. H. Robertson, JP; J. M. Catlett, JP; C. Buchanan, JP; Inman H. Evans, JP.**

<u>May 25, 1869 Court</u>   page 324.
Ordered that **Thomas Smith, John H. Rixey and John S. Mosby** be... empowered and directed to contact for and have erected at as early a date as practicable, a suitable fence enclosing the public grounds between the Clerk's office and the California House, after first advertising for proposals for the enclosure and letting the contract to the lowest bidder.
The questions of disposing of the remains of the old wall and the character of the fence is left to the discretion of the committee.

<u>May 26, 1869 Court</u>   page 327.
The **Court recommends to the Commanding General of this District that William Baker be appointed Constable in the 6th Magisterial District of this County, and that T. R. Wilson be appointed Constable in the 9th District of this County.**
The Court is satisfied that Baker and Wilson are loyal men of good character and qualifications and can take the oath prescribed by the Act of Congress passed July 2, 1862 and that they will qualify to their Commissions if appointed.

<u>June 28, 1869 Court</u>   page 347.
John E. Fletcher, who by an order from the General commanding the first Military District, State of Virginia, has been appointed Overseer of Poor for the 9th District of this County, this day qualified as such by producing to the court a copy of the oath prescribed by an Act of Congress passed July 2, 1862, then and subscribed by him before a Justice of Peace of this County, and taking in open Court the oath to support the Constitution of the United States, the oath of Fidelity to the Commonwealth of Virginia, the anti-dwelling oath and the oath of office.

Fauquier County Minute Book 1867-1869

July 26, 1869 Court   page 357.
James E. Murray produced to the Court evidence of his appointment as a Justice of Peace for this County by the commanding General of the first Military District, State of Virginia, and of his qualifications as such Justice, which are ordered to be filed among the records of the Court.

Upon the motion **of William H. Boyd, Sheriff of Fauquier County, W.A. Boyd qualified as Deputy or Under Sheriff** by taking the following oaths—the oath of Fidelity to the Commonwealth of Virginia, the oath to support the Constitution of the United States, the anti-dwelling oath and the oath of office.

July 26, 1869 Court   page 358.
James H. Bussey, who by order from the Headquarters of the first Military District, State of Virginia, dated July 3, 1869, has been appointed Constable for the 3rd Magisterial District of Fauquier County, to fill the vacancy occasioned by the removal of Robert Willis from office, this day qualified and took the oath of Fidelity to the Commonwealth of Virginia, the oath to support the Constitution of the United States, the anti-dwelling oath and the oath of office.
Thereupon James H. Bussey, together with his sureties, entered into and acknowledged a bond in the penalty of $3,000.00 conditioned and payable as the law directs... and ordered to be recorded.

August 23, 1869 Court   page 375.
John W. Hough, who by order of the Major General commanding the first Military District, State of Virginia, has been appointed Commissioner of Revenue for Fauquier County in District # 2.
This day, he qualified by taking the oath of Fidelity to the Commonwealth of Virginia, the oath to support the Constitution of the United States, the anti-dwelling oath and the oath of office. John W. Hough, together with his securities, who justified as to their sufficiency, entered into a bond in the penalty of $3,000.00, which was ordered to be recorded.

Fauquier County Minute Book 1867-1869

August 23, 1869 Court   page 375.

Ludwell Seaton, alias George L. Seaton, has been appointed Constable in District 9 in this County, by the Major General commanding the first Military District,
He thereupon took the oath of Fidelity to the Commonwealth of Virginia, the oath to support the Constitution of the United States, the anti-dwelling oath and the oath of office.
Ludwell Seaton, alias George L. Seaton, together with his securities, who justified as to their sufficiency, entered into and acknowledged a bond in the penalty of $5,000.00 which was ordered to be recorded.

September 28, 1869 Court   page 402.
James G. Cannon v. Wm. H. Boyd, Sheriff of Fauquier County
The Honorable Lysander Hill, Judge of the 9th Judicial Circuit,
having (in exercise of authority conferred on him as set forth in the order of this Court entered at the last term) entered on the records of the Circuit Court of Fauquier the following order:
William H. Boyd, Sheriff of Fauquier County, having failed to execute a new bond for Sheriff... as required by the order of this Court made on September 15, 1869 – The Court, on September 23, 1869, declares that Wm. H. Boy, as Sheriff, by his failure, is **deemed to have been guilty of a breach of official duty** and hereby orders that he be, and **he is, hereby removed from Office as Sheriff of Fauquier County**.
And this **cause coming on to be heard at this term and the defendant W. H. Boyd having** heretofore **failed, and still failing to give the new bond** required by the Court at its May term 1869 to be given him as Sheriff of Fauquier, the **Court certifies that Boyd is deemed guilty of breach of Official duty** and hereby **declared to be removed from his Office as Sheriff of Fauquier and he is so removed.**

The Court orders **Silas H. Turner not to deliver copies of the Books of the Commissioner of Revenue to Boyd or any of his deputies** but to deep the books in his possession until a new election for Sheriff has been held.

Fauquier County Minute Book 1867-1869

October 2, 1869 Court   page 407
    The Commissioners of Public Buildings this day made their report to the Court setting forth **the condition of the jail... and recommending for its repair.** On consideration of which report, the Court, approving the recommendation, directs the Commissioners to proceed at once to have the necessary repairs made and for that purpose they will expend $275.00 out of the $1,500.00 levied in their hands for repairs of the Court house.
    The Commissioners are also to proceed at once to have the Court house repaired in order that the same may be finished before the winter.
    [NOTE: Warrenton's public buildings had been in a state of disrepair since the 1861-1862 occupation of the town by federal forces.]

October, 9, 1869 Court   page 409.
    William H. Boyd, who by an order dated "Headquarters 18th Division of Virginia, Warrenton October 9, 1869" and filed among the records of this Court, has been "reinstated in Office as Sheriff of Fauquier County, upon filing bond with sufficient security therein in the amount named in the former bond."
    Wm. Boyd qualified, this day, as Sheriff by taking the following oaths, the oath prescribed by the Act of Congress of July 2, 1862, the oath to support the Constitution of the United States, the oath of Fidelity to the Commonwealth of Virginia, the anti-dwelling oath and the oath of office.
    Together with **William M. Hume, Thomas A. Rector, Benjamin Feagans, James E. Murray, Joshua Owens, James S. Thomson, Robert Scott and Severe F. G. Beale, his sureties, who justified as to their sufficiency, Wm. H. Boyd entered into and acknowledged a bond** in the penalty of $30,000.00, in open Court, payable and conditioned as the law directs...

    On the motion of **Wm. H. Boyd, Sheriff of Fauquier County, Wm. H. Hume, Robert Scott, Battle Rector, S.F.G. Beale, R. H. Downman, Horace Pattie and Joseph H. Nelson, qualified as Deputies or under Sheriffs of the County** by taking the following oaths – the oath to support the Constitution of the United States, the oath of Fidelity to the Commonwealth of Virginia, the anti-dwelling oath and the oath of Office.
    The Court is satisfied that they are men of honesty and good demeanor.

Fauquier County Minute Book 1867-1869

<u>October 25, 1869 Court</u>   page 414.
   John Weedon, who by an order from "Headquarters, first Military District, State of Virginia" dated October 2, 1869, has been appointed a Justice of Peace for this County in the 9th Magisterial District, to fill the vacancy caused by the removal of John Carr from Office.
   John Weedon qualified, this day, by taking the oath prescribed by the Act of Congress of July 2, 1862, the oath to support the Constitution of the United States, the anti-dwelling oath and the oath of office.

   On the motion of **William H. Boyd, Sheriff of Fauquier County, Cuthbert Owens qualified as Deputy or Under Sheriff of this County** by taking the oath prescribed by the Act of Congress of July 2, 1862, the oath to support the Constitution of the United States, the anti-dwelling oath and the oath of office.
   The Court is satisfied that he is a man of honesty and good demeanor.

Fauquier County Minute Book 1869-1871

<u>January 25, 1870 Court</u>   page 47.
   Wm. H. Gaines this day **returned to Court fourteen County bonds amounting to $1,500.00,** which fell due January 1, 1870 and **which have been paid off by Gaines.**

<u>March 28, 1870 Court</u>   page 64.
   James Rogers, Clerk of Court, together with T.N. Fletcher and John A. Spilman, his sureties, entered into and acknowledged a bond as such Clerk, in penalty of $10,000.00, as required by Act of General Assembly of Virginia approved March 5, 1870, known as the "Enabling Act."
   Rogers thereupon took the Oath of office prescribed by the Act of Assembly approved March 15, 1870 entitled "An act prescribing the Oath of Office and also an oath in these words: " I do solemnly sear that I have never taken an oath as a Member of Congress, or as an officer of the United States, or as a member of any State Legislature, or as an Executive or Judicial officer of any State, to support the Constitution of the United States, and afterwards engaged in insurrection or rebellion against the same, or given aid or comfort to the enemies thereof. So help me God." And a bond is ordered to be delivered to the Clerk of Circuit Court of this County for recordation.

Fauquier County Minute Book 1869-1871

<u>April 25, 1870 Court</u>   page 83.
Thomas Smith Esq. produced his Commission as Judge of Court under the hand of Gilbert C. Walker, Governor of the State of Virginia, dated April 19, 1870, **together with evidence of his qualification before Samuel H. Crockford, a Notary Public for Fauquier County**, endorsed thereon, which is ordered to be filed.

T.N. Fletcher, appointed Clerk of the Court, is to continue in Office until his successor is duly elected and qualified by taking Oath to support the Constitution of the United States, the anti-dwelling oath and the oath of office.
T.N. Fletcher, together with Wm. H. Gaines, and M. Fletcher his securities, approved by the Court, entered into and acknowledged a bond in penalty of $10,000.00, conditioned as the law directs, which bond is ordered to be delivered to the Clerk of Circuit Court of Fauquier County for recording.

Wm. M. Hume is appointed Sheriff of this County and is to continue in office until his successor shall be regularly elected and qualified according to law.
Hume thereupon qualified by taking the oath of office prescribed by the General Assembly of Virginia ... also an oath in these words: "I do solemnly swear that I have, by Act of Congress of the United States, been relieved from disabilities imposed upon me by the 14th Amendment of the Constitution of the United States. So help me God."
Together with his sureties **Thomas A. Rector, James S. Thomson, R.H. Downman, James E. Murray, Joshua Owens, R. Scott, S.F.G. Beale, Joseph H. Nelson, Wm. Cooke, Cuthbert Owens and Jacob Hume**, who justified as to their sufficiency, **entered into and acknowledged bond** in penalty of $60,000.00, conditioned according to law. The Bond is ordered to be recorded.

<u>August 27, 1870 Court</u>   page 157.
The Court appointed **Dallas P. Gordon** as Assessor for Township of Cedar Run in Fauquier County, he having been elected... but failed to qualify within the time prescribed by law. He is to hold office until a successor is duly elected...

Fauquier County Minute Book 1869-1871

January 25, 1871 Court   page 219.
The Report of **J.M. Forbes, R.W. Payne, and J.V. Brooke, the military committee appointed at the April term of this Court 1861, was this day returned** in obedience to the order of the Court entered at last October term, by which it appears that the sum of $26.25 is due to R.W. Payne.
The Court, having examined the report, confirms it and orders it filed among the papers preserved in the Clerk's office.

Fauquier County Minute Book 1871-1873

May 27, 1872 Court   page 116.
The Court certifies that it appears by sufficient evidence **that Westard Fletcher** is a citizen of this State, that he **lost his leg in the late War**, that he was disabled to such an extent that an artificial leg cannot be used or worn by him.

June 4, 1872 Court   page 137.
The Court certifies that it appears by sufficient evidence that **B.F. Conrad** is a citizen of this State, that he **lost his leg in the late War**, and that he was disabled to such an extent that an artificial leg cannot be used or worn by him and that he has never received an artificial leg from the State of Virginia.

June 24, 1872 Court   page 148.
On the motion of Meredith J. Sanford, the Court certifies that satisfactory evidence has been exhibited to it that **Mary Kernes was a pensioner of the United States, residing at or near Bealeton in the County of Fauquier, State of Virginia, and died on December 19, 1871.**
She left no father, mother, brother or sister and only 5 children: **Mary Ann Heflin, Frances Rives, Eliza Jane Cain, Wm. Kearnes and Sarah Ann Sanford**, who have **given full power of attorney to Meredith Sanford, husband of Sarah Ann Sanford and son-in-law of Mary Kernes decd.**

Fauquier County Minute Book 1871-1873

June 26, 1872 Court   page 157.
On satisfactory evidence produced before the Court by Dallas P. Gordon, the court certifies that **Dallas P. Gordon** is a citizen of the State of Virginia, that he **lost his arm in the late War** and was a citizen of this State at the time of the loss of his arm.
The Court further certifies that Dallas P. Gordon has not received an artificial arm from any other State, the United States, or under the provisions of an Act entitled an act to provide artificial limbs for citizens of this Commonwealth who lost their limbs in the late War, passed January 29, 1867; The Court further certifies that Dallas B. Gordon was so disabled, to such an extent, that an artificial arm cannot be worn or used by him.

January 27, 1873 Court   page 265.
The Court certifies that it appears by evidence that **W. F. Kerfoot** is a citizen of this State, that he **lost his arm in the late War**, and that he is so disabled that the arm furnished him by the State cannot be used or worn.

February 24, 1873 Court   page 276.
The Court certifies that it appears by sufficient evidence that **Charles W. Furr** is a citizen of this State, that he **lost his arm in the late War** and that he has never received an arm from the State of Virginia.

The Court certifies that it appears by sufficient evidence that **Wm. H. Triplett** is a citizen of this State, that he **lost his arm in the late War** and that he has never received an arm from the State of Virginia.

The Court certifies that it appears by sufficient evidence that **Wm. H. Tate** is a citizen of this State, that he **lost his arm in the late War,** and that he was a citizen of Virginia at the time of his loss and that he has never received an arm from the State of Virginia.

February 25, 1873 Court   page 282.
The Court certifies upon evidence produced before it **that Captain Alfred B. Carter** is a citizen of the State of Virginia and resident of this County, that he **lost his right arm in the late War** waged between the United States and the Confederate States; that he was a citizen of this State **at the time he lost his arm and held a Commission as Captain of Co. F, 6th Rgt,. Virginia Cavalry.**

Fauquier County Minute Book 1871-1873

<u>February 25, 1873 Court</u>   page 282. (Cont.)
Captain Carter's arm was amputated in consequence of a wound received in battle; that he has never received an artificial arm from any other State or from the United States, or under provisions of any act of the General Assembly of Virginia, nor has he received any sum of money in lieu thereof either from the State of Virginia or otherwise.

<u>March 25, 1873 Court</u>   page 301.
On the motion of James D. Kirby, the Court certifies that satisfactory evidence has been exhibited to the Court that **John Kirby was a pensioner of the United States, residing at Warrenton in the County of Fauquier, State of Virginia and died February 27, 1873** and that he **left** no relatives nearer than his **widow Cecelia B. Kirby, surviving him.**

<u>May 26, 1873 Court</u>   page 351.
The Court certifies that it appears by sufficient evidence that **George D. Edmonds** is a citizen of this State, that he **lost his arm in the late War**, and that he was a citizen of Virginia at the time of his loss, and that he is disabled to such an extent that an artificial arm cannot be use or worn.

<u>May 26, 1873 Court</u>   page 352.
On the motion of Lucetta Matthew, the Court certifies that satisfactory evidence has been exhibited to it that **Nancy Fletcher was a pensioner of the United States residing at or near Warrenton in the County of Fauquier, State of Virginia, and died March 3, 1873; that she left no father, mother, brother, or sister and only 5 children: Matthias Fletcher, Susan Fletcher, Alethia Fletcher, Nancy Jeffries and Lucetta Matthew.**
The first four children [named above] have united in consent in writing that their **sister Lucetta Matthew, should draw the arrears of pay due to their deceased mother.**

Fauquier County Court Minute Book 1873-1876

<u>May 25, 1874 Court</u>   page 72.
The Court certifies that it appears by sufficient evidence **that George W. Davis** is a citizen of this State, and that he **lost his leg in the late War;**

Fauquier County Court Minute Book 1873-1876

<u>May 25, 1874 Court</u>   page 72. (Cont.)
And that the artificial leg received by Davis, under a former Act of Assembly, is unfit for use and therefore cannot be worn. Davis is, however, wearing an artificial leg of his own procurement.

Fauquier County Court Minute Book 1876-1880

<u>April 24, 1877 Court</u>   page 90.
E.G. Edmonds, came this day, by his Attorney, and **applied to the Court for a Certificate necessary to enable him to procure the commutation for an eye, lost in the late War**, provided for in "An Act to allow commutation for soldiers maimed in War, in lieu of artificial limb and eyes provided by law, approved March 29, 1877."
Thereupon came **L.L. Lomax**, who being duly sworn, stated to the Court that he **was a Brigadier General commanding a Cavalry Brigade of Fitz Lee's Division, Army of Northern Virginia during the late War.**
E.G. Edwards, the applicant, **was a private in Co. A, 6th Rgt., Virginia Cavalry in his Brigade; Edwards lost his left eye by a gunshot wound received while sharpshooting at Mechanicsville on the Chickahominy near Richmond, Virginia, in the spring of 1864, soon after the fatal wounding of General J.E.B. Stuart**; that he was taken from the field to Hospital, in Richmond and as far as he knew, was not thereafter able to rejoin his command; that his eye was totally destroyed; that he has been and continues to be a great sufferer from the loss of his eye; and that he has never been furnished by any State Government, or the United States, with an artificial eye, nor received commutation therefor.
And **E.G. Edmonds stated under oath in open Court**, that he is a citizen of the State of Virginia; that **he lost an eye while in the military service, in the late War, on May 12, 1864;** that he was a citizen of this State at the time of losing his eye; that he has not received an eye or commutation therefor under any of the acts heretofore passed for that purpose; and that he is disabled in such manner as to prevent the use of one eye, in manual labor, induced by wounds received as aforesaid while a soldier in the late war.
Thereupon the Court certifies [to the same] and that further E.G. Edmonds was so disabled... to such an extent that an artificial eye cannot be worn or used by him.

Fauquier County Court Minute Book 1876-1880

<u>May 28, 1877 Court</u>   pages 99-100.

J.N. Shaw applied to the Court for a Certificate necessary to enable him to procure the commutation for an eye lost in the late war, provided for in "An Act to allow commutation for soldiers maimed in the late War, in lieu of artificial limbs and eyes provided by law, approved March 29, 1877."

Thereupon came **John C. Compton**,... duly sworn... **a private, in Co. C of Mosby's command, Captain Wm. H. Chapman, during late War; that the applicant J.N. Shaw was a private in the same Company; that Shaw lost his eye from the effects of a gunshot wound received while in action at the farm of Henry G. Dulany, near Upperville in this County, in the fall of 1864**; that he was **borne from the field to the house of Henry G. Dulany where he remained some days and was then removed to his home in Culpeper County**, where [Compton] soon after visited him; that he [Shaw] did not thereafter rejoin his Company; that his eye is totally destroyed, and that he has never been furnished by any State Government, or the United States, with an artificial eye, nor received commutation therefor.

J.N. Shaw stated to the Court, under oath, that he is a citizen of the State of Virginia; that **he lost an eye, while in military service during the late War, on October 29, 1864**; that he was a citizen of the State of Virginia at the time of losing his eye; that he has not received an eye nor commutation therefor, under any of the Acts heretofore passed for that purpose; and that he is disabled in such manner as to prevent use of one eye, in manual labor, induced by wound received as aforesaid while a soldier in the late War.

The Court certifies [to the same.]

<u>June 25, 1877 Court</u>   pages 107-108.

Charles S. Marshall's Application for Certificate... to procure Commutation of eye lost in the late War, provided for in "An Act to allow commutation for Soldiers, maimed in the War, in lieu of artificial limbs and eyes provided by law, approved March 29, 1877."

Thereupon cam **John M. Jeffries**, who being duly sworn, stated that he is well acquainted with Charles S. Marshall, that he **served in the same company of Infantry with him, that he knows that he was wounded at the fight at Mechanicsville, near Richmond in 1862, and that Wm. S. Marshall lost his left eye [there], the sight thereof being totally destroyed.**

Fauquier County Court Minute Book 1876-1880

<u>June 25, 1877 Court</u>   pages 107-108. (Cont.)

Also came **Captain Wm. C. Marshall**, who being duly sworn, stated that he **was an Artillery Officer and served in Stribling's Battery during the late War; that he knows Charles S. Marshall well; that Charles S. Marshall was wounded in fights around Richmond in 1862.**

Charles S. Marshall, being duly sworn, says that he is a citizen of the State of Virginia, **that he lost an eye while in military service during the late War, in one of the Seven Days fights around Richmond in 1862...** at **Mechanicsville,** that he was a citizen of Virginia at the time of losing his eye, that **he was a private in the 65th Rgt., Virginia Infantry, in Company F, attached to Field's Brigade, A.P. Hill's Division, at the time he lost his eye** that he has not received any eye, nor commutation therefor under any of the Acts heretofore passed for that purpose and that he is disabled in such manner as to prevent the use of one eye in manual labor, evidenced by the wound received aforesaid as a soldier in the late War.

The Court certifies [to the same.]

<u>March 28, 1878 Court</u>   page 207.

Satisfactory evidence was produced before the Court that **Mark Haley was a pensioner of the United States, residing near Warrenton in the County of Fauquier, State of Virginia, that he died September 25, 1873 and that he left a widow Harriet Haley.**

<u>May 28, 1878 Court</u>   page 230.

Satisfactory evidence was this day exhibited to the court, by the oath of Enoch Jeffries, that **Thomas Fletcher was a pensioner of the United States, residing near Warrenton in the County of Fauquier, State of Virginia and that he died June 13, 1876 and that he left a widow Elizabeth Fletcher.**

Fauquier County Court Minute Book 1880-1884

<u>August 23, 1881 Court</u>   page 119.
It appearing to the satisfaction of the Court, by the oaths **of Luther R. Welch and Wm. H.** Lewis, residents of this County, and persons whom the Court certifies as respectable and entitled to credit, **that Thornton Leach, who received a pension under Claim No. 3440, under the Act of February 14, 1871**, and to whom a check for $25.00, No. 194317 dated Knoxville, Tennessee September 14, 1880, drawn by D. T. Boynton United States Pension Agent, on the Assistant Treasurer of the United States, New York, New York, A[3] was issued, **was one and the same as Thornton K. Leach** on **whose estate letters of administration were granted to Jane Leach at the November term 1880, of this Court.**
These facts are ordered to be certified that Jane Leach as Adm[x] of Thornton K. Leach decd., may be enabled to procure payment of the check and disburse the amount thereof as the personal effects of Thornton K. Leach decd.

<u>March 28, 1882 Court</u>   pages 175-176.
In the matter of the **application of Whitfield Peters of Fauquier County, State of Virginia under the act approved 2/14/1882 entitled "An Act to provide commutation to such maimed soldiers, sailors and marines, in lieu of artificial limbs or eyes as may heretofore have received the same under provision of former acts."**
The act provides 1) for those who have not heretofore received limbs or eyes or commutations in money for the same under any act of the General Assembly heretofore passed for that purpose; 2) for those who have been disabled in such a manner as to prevent the use of limbs or eyes in manual labor or otherwise disabled from the performance of manual labor, induced by wounds or surgical operations rendered necessary thereby: 3) for those who have received an artificial limb and upon satisfactory proof that the limb has been worn out or destroyed by accident; and 4) for those who have receive $30.00 under the Act of 2/8/1879.
And the Court being satisfied from proper testimony that the applicant is now, and was at the time he was disabled, a citizenof Virginia; that he was disabled, maimed or wounded or lost his limb or ey in the late war, or in a military corps of this State or during temporary absence form the Commonwealth of Virginia enlisted in the commands of other States; that he has not received an artificial limb from any other State or of the United States which is ordered to be certified to the Auditor of Public Account, together with other facts and testimony of witnesses, sworn and examined in the word and figures following to wit –

Fauquier County Court Minute Book 1880-1884

<u>March 28, 1882 Court</u>   pages 175-176. (Cont.)
Application of Whitfield Peters for wounds received in late war

We the undersigned, **William Smith, Colonel of the 49th Virginia Volunteers and Wm. T. Weaver, private, Company H, 49th Virginia Rgt., hereby certify that Whitfield Peters was a member of Company H, 49th Virginia Rgt. and was with the command at the 1st Battle of Manassas** between the United States forces and the Confederate Army on **July 21, 1861—and there received a wound in the left hand, the use of which has ever since been entirely destroyed for any purpose whatsoever** and from the effect of which disability he has been entirely unable to do any manual labor with the hand and arm.

We further certify that Whitfield Peters is a laboring man, dependent upon his daily exertions for his livelihood and is seriously crippled by his injury in his struggle to support himself and family.
          (signed)   Wm. Smith, late Col., 49th Virginia Volunteers
                    W.T. Weaver
Witness March 28, 1882   R.H. Downman, Clerk

<u>March 28, 1882 Court</u>   page 176.
          On the application of **Wm. E. Ball for commutation for Act approved 12/14/1882...**
          The original certificate of **surgeon R. L. Madison of Orange Court House Hospital was approved by General G. T. Beauregard discharging Ball from service as a man disabled by wounds.**
          This day Wm. Edward Ball of Scott district, Fauquier County Virginia personally appeared before me in open Court and made oath that he enlisted in the War between the United States and Confederate States and was wounded and discharged because of wounds from service, that the wounds disabled him no only from military service but from manual labor and that the disability has continued to this day and now exists, that he has never received any from the Commonwealth; Bull further avers that he was a member of Company C of the 8th Virginia Rgt. Given under my hand 3/28/1882.
          (signed)   R.H. Downman, Clerk
W.M. Griffith of Fauquier County, Virginia personally appeared before me in open Court and made oath that he well knew the applicant Wm. Edward Ball, that he now lives and has lived near him for several years and knows him to have been disabled by wounds and that he is now incapable of manual labor...

Fauquier County Court Minute Book 1880-1884

March 28, 1882 Court   page 176-177.
Application of Wm. Edward Ball for commutation for wound received in late war

The wounds were received in the recent war between the United and Confederate States. Given under my hand 3/28/1882.
(signed) R. H. Downman, Clerk.

B.T. Hurst... appeared... in open Court and made oath that he is a citizen of Fauquier County, Virginia; that **he well knows Wm. Edward Ball of Fauquier County; that he was a soldier in the same company during the Confederate and Union war; that he knows Ball was desperately wounded in the war and discharged because of the wounds,** that he lives now and has lived near him ever since the recent war and he knows that Ball has continued from the time of his wound to the present day, disabled and incapable of performance of manual labor. Ball has never received any artificial limb or commutation from the State.

April 25, 1882 Court   pages 183-184.
The **application of Daniel Burr Harrison for commutation under the Act approved 2/14/1882...**
Wm. H. Payne of Fauquier County, Virginia certified that he knew Daniel Burr Harrison of Fauquier County; **Harrison was a private soldier in Payne's Brigade... and was wounded, in Payne's presence, in action. His wound was a desperate one and caused the loss of his right eye.** He has been a sufferer from it ever since and is unable to bear hard labor.
"My opinion is that Mr. Harrison is in every way entitled to the Commutation or allowance, whatever it may be, provided by the Legislature. To the best of my knowledge he has never received anything from the State. **He was ignorant of the law until informed by me and when his application was approved by the Court and forwarded it was said the appropriations had been exhausted."**
(signed) W. H. Payne 4/3/1882.

Fauquier County Court Minute Book 1880-1884

April 25, 1882 Court   page 184.
The **Application of G. W. Davis of Fauquier County, Virginia for commutation under the Act approved 2/14/1882...**
George W. Davis this day appeared in open Court and made oath that heretofore he received from the State of Virginia, upon Certificate of the County Court of Fauquier County, an artificial leg, which he wore until it became useless; that he has bought several since that date, and no asks a new artificial leg or the commutation allowed by law; that he lost a leg in the late war in the service of the Confederate States; and that record of the fact is now on file in the State Auditors office at Richmond.
(signed) G. W. Davis

May 24, 1882 Court   page 195.
The Application of Charles W. Furr of Fauquier County, Virginia for commutation under the Act of 2/14/1882...
R.Taylor Scott, in open Court, stated that the applicant Charles W. Furr is personally known to him; that he enlisted Furr in his own Volunteer Company, which was afterwards assigned to the 8th Rgt., Virginia Infantry, Colonel Eppa Hunton, in the summer of 1861; that Furr served in the Company and Rgt. during the period of the late war; that Furr remained in active service until the spring of 1862.
When, in the battles around Richmond City, viz., that of Gaines Mill, Furr was wounded in his right arm amputated near the shoulder and upon his recovery, Furr was detailed from the County and discharged duty as a "detailed soldier" until the surrender at Appomattox. Scott stated further that Furr has suffered and still suffers severely from the loss of his limb, that he is a citizen of the County of Fauquier and of this Commonwealth and a most deserving man and a brave soldier; and that he has received no artificial limb and no commutation for loss of his limb.

May 24, 1882 Court pages 196-197.
On the **Application of George H. Robinson of Fauquier County,** ⁀⁀⁀⁀⁀**a for commutation under the Act of 2/14/1882...**
"Markham, May 8, 1882. Judge Shumate. Dear Sir. George H. Robinson was a member of my company during the war and I know that fact that he was disabled by rheumatism and discha⁀⁀⁀ ' ‾
‾   ‾   ‾   ⁀⁀⁀ :ause. Respectfully, (signed) Wm. C. Marshall, Captain, Fauquier Artillery."

Fauquier County Court Minute Book 1880-1884

May 24, 1882 Court pages 196-197.(Cont.)
Application of George H. Robinson for commutation...

Louisa Ct Ho. Va. May 5, 1882. I hereby certify that **George Robinson of Fauquier County Virginia was during the latter part of 1864, sent before a medical board, who pronounced him maimed and disabled and unfit for active military service.**
(signed) W. T. Meade, formerly Captain and A.Q.M. Arty. Ord. Train, Army N.V^a.

October 28, 1884 Court   pages 468-469.
    Resolution by members of the Bar and officers of the Circuit and County Court presented to the Court **regarding the death of Major [Rice W.] Payne...**
... the bar of Fauquier Has lost a valued member...
Note by the Court from Judge John R. Turner
    ... had the good fortune to enjoy the uninterrupted friendship of the deceased for 40 years of my life and learned to appreciate the many admirable traits of his character... As a lawyer, so unremitting and faithful was he, in attention to the business of his clients, that, I doubt, if during his whole career, he spent one listless idle hour at places of public resort... his intercourse with his brother members of the bar was distinguished by a high degree of courtesy... A faithful lawyer, a ripe scholar, a genial and courteous gentleman, his death has created a void at this bar and in this community which it will not be easy to fill...

Fauquier County Court Minute Book 1884-1888

February 24, 1885 Court   pages 40-41.
Resolution by members of the Bar and officers of the Circuit and County Court presented to the Court **on the death of Wm. H. Gaines**, for many years the **presiding magistrate of the Court of Fauquier County and Judge for six years...**

Fauquier County Court Minute Book 1884-1888

October 27, 1885 Court   page 140.

It appears to the satisfaction of the Court, upon ample testimony of witnesses produced in open Court, and upon the personal knowledge of the Judge of this Court, that **Sally Innes Bartels, nee Forbes, late wife of Herman Bartels, died while a resident of Fauquier County, State of Virginia, in the U.S.A. on Tuesday September 13, 1881**; it is ordered that the facts, so proved, and known to the Judge of this Court, be entered of record.

October 27, 1885 Court   page 141.

Satisfactory evidence was produced to the Court that **Sarah Padgett, the identical person alleged to be entitled to an accrued pension, as the widow of Dempsey Padgett decd., died at Warrenton, Fauquier County, Virginia within the jurisdiction of this Court on August 24, 1885, leaving no minor child** and without sufficient assets to defray the **expenses of her last sickness and burial**; that the same **were borne by G. W. Meetze,** and that the itemized accounts therewith attached marked [left blank] are just and true and that there is justly due G. W. Meetze above the assets of decedent's estate the sum of $16.68.00 on account of the necessary expenses of her last sickness.

February 26, 1886 Court   page 181.

On the **Application of Thomas A. Lee, a disabled soldier for commutation money...**

The Court carefully considering the written application of Thomas A. Lee verified by his oath and the evidence adduced in support of his application is of the opinion that Lee is entitled to aid as a disabled soldier and directs the application and all the evidence in the case to be certified to the Auditor of Public Accounts.

February 26, 1886 Court   page 181.

    D.F. Brown v. Commonwealth of Virginia}

    Julius A. Pilcher v. same}   **Applications for Commutation Money**

    Jere Heflin v. same}

The Court carefully considering the written applications of the applicants, verified by their oaths and evidence adduced in support of the same, is of the opinion that applicants are entitled to aid as disabled Confederate Soldiers and direct the applications and all evidence in each case to be certified to the Auditor of Public Accounts.

Fauquier County Court Minute Book 1884-1888

April 30, 1886 Court   page 202.
It appearing to the satisfaction of the Court that **G.B. Dawson is physically disabled**, it is ordered that he be relieved from the capitation tax and also from work on public roads.

May 1, 1886 Court   page 203.
In **James Mahorney's Application for aid under an Act of the General Assembly approved February 25, 1884**, entitled an Act to give Aid to the Citizens of Virginia wounded and maimed during the late war while serving as soldiers or marines.
The Court having maturely considered the **written application of Mahorney, verified by his oaths and the evidence adduced in support of the Application, is of the opinion that the applicant is entitled to aid** under the act and directs the application and all the evidence in the case certified to the Auditor of Public Accounts.

May 28, 1886 Court   page 214.
On the **Application of Nelson Farmer for Aid under the Act of the General Assembly approved February 25, 1884**...
The Court, having carefully considered the **written application of Nelson Farmer, verified by his oath and the evidence adduced in support of his application, is of the opinion that the applicant is entitled to aid**... and directs the application and all the evidence in the case to be certified to the Auditor of Public Accounts.

September 27, 1887Court   page 350.
The Court requires a bond of competent physicians, consisting of three, to be appointed by the board of Supervisors of Fauquier County, to certify, in accordance with law as to the disabilities of applicants as disabled soldiers or marines, under the Act of Assembly (Extra Session 1887) approved May 23, 1887.

November 30, 1887 Court   page 377.
On the application of **Captain A. B. Carter for aid under Act of General Assembly approved May 23, 1887** entitled "An Act to require proof of disability in order to obtain aid as a disabled soldier or marine, wounded and maimed during the late war.

Fauquier County Court Minute Book 1884-1888

November 30, 1887 Court   page 377.
The Application of Captain A. B. Carter for Aid (Cont.)
       The **Court, having carefully considered the written application of Captain A. B. Carter, verified by his oath, the Certificate of the Board of Physicians and other evidence adduced in support of the application, is of the opinion that Captain A. B. Carter is entitled to aid under the Act,...** The Court, from proof adduced before it, certifies 1) that Applicant is a citizen of Virginia; 2) that he was [a citizen] during the late war;... 3) that he was engaged as a soldier in military service of Virginia; 4) that he **lost his right arm from surgical operations rendered necessary by a wound received in battle**; 5) that he is dependent on physical labor... for his subsistence; and 6) that he has not, within five years, received an artificial limb or ey, or commutation money form this State.

April 23, 1888 Court   page 420.
       The **several applications of Thomas A. Lee, Ludwell F. Patton, Robert Smith, Nelson P. Farmer, Evan Griffith, Albert Ballard, Robert McCormick for aid under provisions of an Act to give aid** to soldiers, sailors and Marines of Virginia maimed and disabled in the War between the States and to the widows of soldiers +c who lost their lives in the war in military service **approved March 5, 1888, were this day filed in this Court.**
       And it is ordered to be entered of record upon the Minute Book of this Court that the applications are severally allowed – which is accordingly done.

April 26, 1888 Court   page 423.
       The **several applications of D.B. Harrison, J.M. Moore, Charles H. James, Francis E. Jones, Sibia Jones, Harriet A. Coppage for aid under the provisions of an Act to give aid to Soldiers,** sailors or Marines of Virginia maimed and disabled in the War between the States and to the widows of soldiers +c who lost their lives in the war in military service **approved March 5, 1888, were this day filed in this Court.**
       And it is ordered to be entered of record on the Minute Book of this Court that these applications are severally allowed – which is accordingly done.

Fauquier County Court Minute Book 1884-1888

<u>May 29, 1888 Court</u>   page 431.
The **several applications of D.B. Harrison, D.G. Brown, Lucretia Payne, Eliza J. Anderson and Delila Dennis, for aid under provisions of Act to give aid to Soldiers**, sailors or marines of Virginia maimed and disabled in the War between the States **and to the widows of soldiers** +c who lost their lives in the War in Military service approved March 5,1888, **were this day filed in this Court**.
And it is ordered to be entered of record on the Minute Book of this Court that these applications are severally allowed – which is accordingly done. [MARGIN NOTE: "Mailed to Aud^r, Marye May 31"—88]

<u>June 25, 1888 Court</u>   pages 435-436.
The **several applications of Jno. McConchie and Elizabeth A. Hanback for aid under provisions of Act to give aid to soldiers**, tc maimed and disabled during the late war between the States, **and to widows of soldiers** +c who lost their lives in military service approved March 5, 1888, **were this day filed in this Court**.
And it is ordered to be entered of record on the Minute Book of this Court that the applications are severally allowed – which is accordingly done.

<u>July 24, 1888 Court</u>   page 444.
The application of Leona Mason for aid under the provisions of an Act to give aid to soldiers +c maimed and disabled during the late war between the States and **to widows of soldiers** +c who lost their lives in military service approved March 5, 18888, **was this day filed in this Court**.
And it is ordered to be entered of record on the Minute Book of this Court that the application is allowed – which is accordingly done.

<u>July 27, 1888 Court</u>   page 446.
The **applications of George C. Robinson and Mary Ann Rutherford, for aid under provisions of an Act to give aid to soldiers** +c maimed and disabled during the late war between the **States and to widows of soldiers** +c who lost their lives in military service approved March 5, 1888, **were this day filed in this Court**.
And it is ordered entered of record on the Minute Book of this Court that the applications are allowed – which is accordingly done.

Fauquier County Court Minute Book 1884-1888

<u>July 27, 1888 Court</u>   pages 448-449.
**The application of Polly Ann Woodward for aid under the
provisions of an Act... to give aid to widows of soldiers
+c...approved March 5, 1888, was this day filed in this Court.**
And it is ordered entered of record on the Minute Book of this Court
that the application is allowed—which is accordingly done.

Fauquier County Court Minute Book 1888-1892

<u>June 24, 1889 Court</u>   page 86.
**The application of Van Buren Costello for aid under provisions
of Act to give aid to soldiers +c... approved March 5, 1888, was this
day filed in this Court.**
And it is ordered entered of record on the Minute Book of this Court
that the application is allowed – which is accordingly done.

<u>June 27, 1891 Court</u>   page 319.
**The applications of Henry F. Edwards, Robert E. Embrey and
Dennis Kelly for aid under provisions of an Act to give aid to
soldiers +c... approved March 5, 1888, were this day filed with this
Court.**
And it is ordered entered of record on the Minute Book of this Court
that the applications are allowed – which is accordingly done.

<u>June 29, 1891 Court</u>   page 322.
**It appearing to the satisfaction of the Court that W.E. Ball is over 60
years of age and not able to work on account of wounds received
during the late war, he is relieved from payment of capitation tax and
other taxes.**

<u>July 31, 1891 Court</u>   page 331.
**The application of Jesse Brown for aid under provisions of Act
to give aid to soldiers +c... approved March 5, 1888, was this day
filed in this Court.**
And it is ordered to be entered of record on the Minute Book of this
Court that the application is allowed – which is accordingly done.

Fauquier County Court Minute Book 1893-1897

<u>November 27, 1894 Court</u>   page 213.
   The application of Janet C. **Weaver for aid under provisions of an
Act to give Aid to soldiers +c... and to their widows, disabled and
killed during the War between the States, as approved March 5, 1888,
was this day filed in this Court.**
   And it is ordered to be entered of record on the Minute Book of this
Court that the application is allowed – which is accordingly done.
[MARGIN NOTE: "Delvd to Judge 27 Nov. 94"]

<u>December 28, 1896 Court</u>   page 441.
   The **application of John W. Waddell for aid under the provisions
of an Act to give aid to soldiers** and marines of Virginia maimed and
disabled during the war between the States +c **approved March 5, 1888,
was this day filed in this Court.**
   And it is ordered to be entered of record on the Minute Book of this
Court that the application is allowed – which is accordingly done.

Fauquier County Court Minute Book 1897-1902

<u>May 24, 1897 Court</u>   page 3.
   Ludwell F. Patton of Cedar Run District... being old and infirm and
unable to work ... **[is] exonerated from payment of the Capitation tax.**

<u>October 2, 1897 Court</u>   pages 48-50.
**Excerpts from the resolutions and comments of members of the bar
and the Judge of the Court on the death of R. Taylor Scott.**
   • R.Taylor Scott was a member of the Fauquier bar and
      Attorney General of Virginia. He **died at his home in Warrenton
      on August 4, 1897.**
   • Scott was **born March 10, 1834 in Fauquier County, the
      son of the Hon. Robert Eden Scott and grandson of the Hon.
      John Scott who was, for many years the Judge of this
      Judicial Circuit and one of the Judges of the General Court.**
   • He graduated from the University of Virginia in 1856 and went
      into law with his father; he was licensed to practice in 1857.
   • **During the late war, R. Taylor Scott served as a Captain in
      the Regiment commanded by then-Colonel (later Brigadier
      General) Eppa Hunton and afterwards served as
      Quartermaster with the rank of Major.**

Fauquier County Court Minute Book 1897-1902

<u>October 2, 1897 Court</u>   pages 48-50. (Cont.)
Excerpts from the resolutions and comments of members of the bar and the Judge of the Court on the death of R. Taylor Scott.

- **After the war, he resumed his practice of law in Warrenton, forming, in 1866, a partnership with James V. Brooke** under the name of Brooke & Scott. **This partnership continued for 27 years.**

- He **represented Fauquier as a "prominent and useful member" of the State Convention of 1867, the House of Delegates in 1881.**

- **In 1889 he was elected Attorney General and reelected to that office in 1893.**

- Scott **married Fanny C. Carter, daughter of R.H. Carter in 1858. His son R. Carter Scott, 2 daughters and wife survive him.** R. Carter Scott now fills his father's unexpired term as Attorney General.

- As a man, he was "intelligent brave honest generous and sincere. His hand was ever open to every appeal of genuine charity. He was indulgent towards the foibles of his fellow men but intolerant of what was mean. He was a loving husband a devoted father and a faithful friend... he added the4 tender graces of a christian life, free from the taint of ostentation or Pharisee pride..."

- "Money making was held by him subordinated to the higher aims of the true lawyer's ambition. He was emmently [sic] methodical, each matter of business was made to await its turn, this habit may not have been consistent with speed but it was conducive to accuracy, conclusions thus formed were held by a strong tenure and enforced by vigorous argument

Excerpts from comments from the Judge of the County Court on the death of R. Taylor Scott

- Robert Taylor Scott's immediate ancestors on both sides were distinguished for high civic virtue and great legal talent.

- "A short time before his death, while conversing with him on his prospects for re-nomination for [Attorney General] I was impressed with his lofty bearing and attitude on that question. He regarded with deepest scorn the intrigues and combinations so frequent in our day by which conventions thwart the fair expression of the popular will. He loathed the trick and detestable manifestation of conventions.

Fauquier County Court Minute Book 1897-1902

October 2, 1897 Court   pages 50-51. (Cont.)
Excerpts from the resolutions and comments of members of the bar and the Judge of the Court on the death of R. Taylor Scott.

- These high principles were instilled into him by his early training and lost none of their force with advancing years.

Death is fast depleting the ranks of such men. As each one departs society feels more keenly its loss. It then realizes in all its force that the great need of our day is more men of this high type... I shall always regard it as among the proudest and most cherished recollections of my life that I enjoyed the friendship and esteem of such a man..."

February 28, 1898 Court   page 95.
The applications of Lewis Cropp and Charles Humphrey for aid under provisions of an Act to give aid to soldiers +c... approved March 5, 1888, were this day filed in this Court.

And it is ordered entered on the Minutes of this Court that the applications are allowed – which are accordingly done.

April 25, 1898 Court   page 117.
The application of James Gray for aid under provisions of an Act to give aid to soldiers +c... approved March 5, 1888, was this day filed in this Court.

And it is ordered entered on the Minutes of this Court that the application is allowed – which is accordingly done. [MARGIN NOTE: "Sent Aud. Apl 28' 98"]

In accordance with provisions of an Act of the General Assembly approved March 3, 1898 entitled an Act **for relief of Luther R. Ashby, a wounded Confederate soldier, the Court certifies that it has examined into the condition of Luther R. Ashby, a confederate soldier**; that he was true and loyal to Virginia through the war; that he is now **afflicted and incapacitated from manual labor as the result of rheumatism contracted during the War in prison; and that he is needy and poor and should receive aid from the State of Virginia.** [MARGIN NOTE: "Sent Aud. Apl 28 1898"]

Fauquier County Court Minute Book 1897-1902

April 25, 1898 Court   page 117.
In accordance with provisions of an Act of the General Assembly approved March 4, 1898 Chapter 932... for relief of Jno. R. Groves, the Court certifies the facts stated in the application and affidavit are true and were fully proven by the oaths of W.B.Thompkins and R.W. Fisher, Confederate Soldiers.
And it appearing that this Court allowed the pension of Jno. R. Groves on March 28, 1898 under the act of March 5, 1888 and has certified the same to the Auditor, it is ordered that the papers together with a copy of this order be certified to the Auditor of Public Accounts.
[MARGIN NOTE: See order 28 Mar 98. Co. sent Aud. April 28 98"]

December 26, 1898 Court   page 181.
Excerpts from resolutions and comments on the death of Charles T. Green.

- Charles T. Green was born at Millwood, Clarke County, Virginia on September 11, 1819, the son of Moses Green. His father moved to Fauquier around 1825 and took up residence near Paris, Virginia.
- While a young man, Charles Green served as a Deputy Sheriff for Fauquier County. He came to Warrenton in 1843 and was a Deputy Clerk of the County Court for several years. While in the Clerk's office, he read law and was admitted to the bar in May 1849.
- Green was a lawyer of the old school, well grounded in the principles of his profession acquired by patient and persevering study without the aid of a college or law school... He was a solid lawyer... a man of strong convictions and outspoken in his views.
- In 1877 he was elected to the State Legislature.
- He became a member of the Baptist Church early in life.
- He was an old line Whig until the War broke out in 1861. "His health forbade his services in the army by he was an earnest and patriotic believer in the Confederate cause and did all he could to promote its success.

Fauquier County Court Minute Book 1897-1902

<u>December 26, 1898 Court</u>   page 182.
Excerpts from Resolutions and comments on death of James V. Brooke.

- **James V. Brooke died at his home in Warrenton on October 9, 1898. He was the son of William and Jeanne Morrison Brooke and born October 10, 1824.**
- He received his early education at Fredericksburg, his childhood home, at a private school. At age 18, he entered the office of the Hon. R.C.L. Moncure as a student of law for a year. Then he removed to Warrenton and worked for Samuel Chilton, where he finished his studies. He was admitted to the Fauquier bar before he was 20 years old.
- **He married Mary E. Norris, daughter of Thaddeus Norris May 23, 1844; the couple had 6 children – Wm. T, Richard N., Jeannie M., Frank C., James V., and Nannie A.** All except Nannie A. survived him.
- In politics he was a follower of Henry Clay.
- **In 1862, he entered the army as a Captain of an Artillery Company he raised. He received a wound in the ankle, fracturing it. He served at the Battle of Fredericksburg. In 1863, being disabled, he was elected to the State Legislature.**
- After the war, he became a Conservative Democrat.
- **In 1871, Brooke was elected to the Legislature and served there from 1871-1873. He was chosen to serve in the State Senate in 1874.**
- "he confined himself closely to the practice of his profession, being engaged in many important cases, both criminal and civil. Mr. Brooke's public life was prominently linked with three of the most important epochs in State history – the Secession Movement, the period immediately after reconstruction, making necessary the revision and renovation of the State Code and lastly the agitation known as the 'Readjuster Period'.
- He joined the Presbyterian Church in 1844.
- He was involved with three important cases:
  - the Bolling-Lersner case which was argued before the United States Supreme Court
  - the Hixson Will case in Loudoun County, Virginia
  - Litigation involving large amounts of property in Washington D.C. still pending in the United States Supreme Court.

Fauquier County Court Minute Book 1897-1902

January 23, 1899 Court   page 185.

The **application of George R. Sealock for aid** under provisions of an act... to give aid to soldiers +c... approved March 5, 1888, **was filed in this Court.**

And it is ordered to be entered in the Minutes of the proceedings thereof that the application is allowed – which is accordingly done.

January 28, 1899 Court   page 191.

The **application of J.W.Canard for aid** under provisions of an act... to give aid to soldiers +c... approved March 5, 1888, **was filed in Court and approved** and is therefore certified to the Auditor of Public Accounts in accordance with law.

March 27, 1899 Court   page 201.

The **application of John R. Groves, disabled Confederate Soldier for an increase of pension** allowed him by Act of Assembly passed March 3, 1888 – See Acts 1887-88, page 469 sworn to by John R. Groves and John P. Summerton and Nancy Groves, accompanied by a Certificate from John P. Summerton, 1719 T. Street, NW, Washington DC and C.H. Willingham of Washington City sworn to before a Notary Public of that City.

It appears to the satisfaction of the Court from other sources that the allegations contained therein are true and John R. Groves is totally disabled from manual labor, that he has no rest from pain and is constantly confined to bed.

The **Court allows an increase of Pension to total disability** and further orders same to be certified to the Auditor of Public Accounts together with all the papers connected therewith. [MARGIN NOTE: "sent all papers + Co. order Mar 29' 99 to Aud."]

The **applications of James A. Speer, R.S. Allison and Wm. J. Taylor, Confederate soldiers disabled during the late War between the States, for aid** under provisions of an Act to give aid to soldiers +c... approved March 5, 1888, **were filed in this Court and** being duly sworn to and witnesses examined, **were severally approved** and ordered certified to the Auditor of Public Account in accordance with law. [MARGIN NOTE: "Sent to Aud. Mar. 29' 99"]

Fauquier County Court Minute Book 1897-1902

April 24, 1899 Court   page 205.
The **application of Robert F. Heflin for an increase of** Pension as a soldier of the Confederate States – appearing to the Court that the **Pension was allowed to him by this Court on May 23, 1898 for partial disability.**
And it further appearing from **a written affidavit of R.C. Burch M.D. and others that Robert F. Heflin is totally and entirely disabled from manual labor and that his ankle and knee are both dislocated upon the least exertion** and that the same results from wounds received during the War between the States.
It is hereby certified to the Auditor of Public Accounts that the disability is total and that Robert F. Heflin is entitled to an increase in Pension. [MARGIN NOTE: "Sent to Aud. Apl 27' 99"]

April 24, 1899 Court   page 207.
The **applications of George Conner and F.M. Foley, Confederate soldiers** -- disabled from the effects of wounds received during the late war between the States – **for aid** under provisions of Act to give aid to soldiers +c.... approved March 5, 1888, **were filed in this Court and** being duly sworn to and witnesses examined, were **severally approved** and ordered certified to the Auditors of Public Accounts in accordance with law.

May 28, 1900 Court   page 293.
In accordance with an Act of the General Assembly approved March 7, 1800 for the relief of John Creel, a Confederate soldier, the Court certifies that John Creel was true and loyal to Virginia during the war; that **he is now afflicted and helpless and by reason of age and decrepitude is unable to perform any manual labor and that he is needy and very poor and should receive aid from the State of Virginia.**

In accordance with an Act of General Assembly approved March 7, 1900 for the relief of Vincent Kerns, a Confederate soldier, the Court certifies from evidence provided before it that **Vincent Kerns** was a true and loyal soldier to Virginia during the war; that he is **now afflicted and diseased and incapacitated from manual labor, the results of hardship endured during the war and that he is needy and poor and should receive aid from the State of Virginia.**

Fauquier County Court Minute Book 1897-1902

<u>May 28, 1900 Court</u>   page 293. (Cont.)
In accordance with an Act of the General Assembly approved March 7, 1900 for the relief of Mattie Gordon, widow of Dallas P. Gordon, a Confederate soldier, member of Company H, 4th Rgt. Virginia Cavalry, the Court certifies that Dallas P. Gordon was a Confederate soldier, that he was true and loyal to Virginia during the War, and that Mattie Gordon is needy and poor and should receive aid from the State of Virginia.

In accordance with an Act of the General Assembly approved March 7, 1900 for the relief of H.C. Mason, Lafanty Ball and Frederick Embrey, Confederate soldiers, the Court certifies that they were true and loyal to the State of Virginia during the war, that they are now afflicted and disabled and incapacitated for manual labor and that they are needy and poor and should receive aid from the State of Virginia.

<u>May 29, 1900 Court</u>   pages 294-295.
The applications of Ellen K. Taylor, Adeline L. Anderson, Mary M. Barber, Edmond T. James, Mrs. Mary Emily Fletcher, Asenath Johnson, John B. Putman, G. Allen Miller, Bernard Oliver, Nimrod Glascock, Joshua T. Kemper, Wm. H. Riley, John J. Kemper, Charles W. Fields, Wm. M. Leach, Charles P. Bragg for Pensions, with the certificate of the Chairman of the Confederate Pension Board of Fauquier County that they have been approved by the Board thereon endorsed, were severally presented to the Court.
And the Clerk of this Court is directed to certify a copy of this order to the Auditor of Public Accounts. [MARGIN NOTE: "sent 30 May 1900"]

<u>June 26, 1900 Court</u>   page 301.
Applications of Nelson P. Farmer, Mrs. May L. Rector, Daniel F. Ball, Aquilla Randall, Silas B. Hanback, Mrs. Lucy E. Oliver, James E. Heflin, Mrs. Lucy A. Doores, P.H. Riley, E.S. Anderson, Richard Hewitt, Samuel D. Reid for Pensions, with the certificate of the Chairman of the Confederate Pension board of Fauquier County that they have been approved by the board thereon endorsed, was presented to the Court.
And the Clerk of this Court is directed to certify a copy of this order to the auditor of Public Accounts. [MARGIN NOTE: "Sent to Aud. 26 Jun 1900"]

Fauquier County Court Minute Book 1897-1902

<u>June 30, 1900 Court</u>   page 302.
     The applications of James H. Moffett, C.P. Smith, Wm. E.
Swayne, N.R. Mooney, John F. Sullivan, W.W. Embrey, Mary M.
Sanders, Fannie Cook, J.R. Shirley, J.T. Patton, C.W. Holtzclaw, W.R.
Soaper for Pensions, with the certificate of the Chairman of the
Confederate Pension Board of Fauquier County that they have been
approved by the Board thereon endorsed, were presented to the Court.
     And the Clerk of this Court is directed to certify a copy of this order to
the Auditor of Public Accounts. This order was omitted on June 27, 1900
by overlooking papers, the same having been filed with the Clerk on June
2, 1900. [MARGIN NOTE: "sent July 5, 1900"]

<u>July 23, 1900 Court</u>   page 306.
     The applications of M.F. Burgess (Auburn), Mrs. Sallie M. Wood
(Somerville), Adolphus Tavenner (Delaplane), Joseph Conner
(Mosby), Thaddeus Gray (Ada), John E. Williams (Markham), Thomas
P. Walden (Bealeton), A.J. Stribling (Morrisville) for Pensions, with
the certificate of the Chairman of the Confederate Pension Board of
Fauquier County, that they have been approved by the Board thereon
endorsed, were presented to the Court.
     And the Clerk of this Court is directed to certify copies of this order to
the Auditor of Public Accounts. [MARGIN NOTE: "SENT 25 July 1900"]

<u>July 28, 1900 Court</u>   page 309.
     The applications of Lucinda Kennard (the Plains), Nancy E.
Weaver (Orlean), Albert Groves (Upperville), Albert O. Sudduth (the
Plains), William R. Soule (Mosby), David Carper (Hume) for
Pensions, with the certificate of the Chairman of the Confederate
Pension Board of Fauquier County that [they] have been approved
by the Board thereon endorsed, was presented to the Court.
     And the Clerk of this Court is directed to certify a copy of this order to
the Auditor of Public Accounts. [MARGIN NOTE: "Sent July 28, 1900"]

<u>April 22, 1900 Court</u>   page 358.
     The application of Daniel C. Herrington (Ada) and Joseph Ballard
(Hitch) for Pensions with the Certificate of the Chairman of the
Confederate Pension Board of Fauquier County that they have been
approved by the Board thereon endorsed, were presented to the Court.
     And the Clerk of this Court is directed to certify a copy of this order to
the Auditor of Public Accounts. [MARGIN NOTE: "Sent to Aud. 23 inst."]

Fauquier County Court Minute Book 1897-1902

June 23, 1901 Court   page 383.
The application of John W. Hurst (near Rectortown) for a pension with the certificate of the Chairman of the Confederate Pension Board of Fauquier County that it has been approved by the Board thereon endorsed, was presented to the Court.

And the Clerk of this Court is directed to certify a copy of this order to the Auditor of Public Accounts. [MARGIN NOTE: "S^{nt} Aud. 24 July 1901"]

November 26, 1901 Court   page 412.
The application of L.M. Manuel (Morrisville) and Arthur Boleyn (Remington) for Pensions with the certificate of the Chairman of the Confederate Pension Board of Fauquier County that [they] had been approved by the Board thereon endorsed, was presented to the Court.

And the Clerk of this Court is directed to certify a copy of this order to the Auditor of Public Accounts.

Fauquier County Court Minute Book 1902-1904

January 30, 1904 Court   page 147.
Excerpts from the Resolutions passed by Members of the Fauquier Bar at the retirement of C.M. White as Judge of the County Court since 1898.

[NOTE: Judge White's retirements was occasioned by the abolition of the County Court system in the new State Constitution.]

"... we will cherish the recollection of [Judge White's] many personal qualities which during his term of service have rendered the intercourse between bench and bar kind and cordial...

The **passing**, by virtue of the State Constitution of the time honored institution **of the County court, and with it the ancient office of County Clerk** which in Fauquier County for years past has been filled by men of conspicuous ability, but by none with more honorable credit to himself and satisfaction to his constituents than by the **present incumbent of that office M.A.R. Bartenstein, whose career in this Office first as assistant and then as Clerk now covers a period of more than twenty years**, being an occasion which we are not content should pass without some expression of appreciation upon our part..."

Surname Given Name	Page	Surname Given Name	Page

Surname Given Name	Page	Surname Given Name	Page
McCabe, Mary, widow of James	17	Morgan, Wm. J.	55, 58.
McClanahan, David W.	35	Mosby, John S.	50, 60.
McClanahan, Margaret E. (Utterback)	35	Murray, James E.	61, 63, 65.
McClanahan, Sarah (widow of Wm.)	6, 7.	Myers, ---- (Tennison)	13
McClanahan, Wm. decd., (Rev. War Pensioner); death certified	6	Negroes, Free Male, impressed for public service	43
McClanahan, Wm. decd., (invalid US Pensioner); death certified	7	Nelson, Benjamin	5
McConchie, John, application for aid approved	80	Nelson, Joseph H.	63, 65.
McCormick, Elizabeth (Claggett)	10	Nelson, Wm. decd., (Rev. War officer); Heirs	5
McCormick, Mary (Roe)	11	Newby, Robert C.	42
McCormick, Robert, application for aid approved	79	Newhouse, S.H.	55
McCormick, Thomas	10	Oliver, Bernard, application for pension approved	89
McCormick, Wm.	11	Oliver, Lucy E., application for pension approved	89
McMullin, Mary (Roach)	12	Ostrander, L.F. (patroller)	38
Meade, W.T.	76	Owens, Cuthbert	64, 65.
Michie, John W.	40	Owens, Joshua	63, 65.
Michie, Mildred A.	40	Padgett, Sarah (US Pensioner); identity certified	77
Miller, G. Miller, application for pension approved	89	Parr, A.J.	58
Mitchell, R.T.	55	Patten, George W.	35
Moffett, James H., application for pension approved	90	Patten, Harriet H. (Lipscomb)	35
Mooney, N.R., application for pension approved	90	Patterson, John H.	35
Moore, Elizabeth (Horner)decd., Heirs	27	Patterson, Maria H. (Whiting)	35
Moore, J.M., application for aid approved	79	Pattie, Horace	50, 63.
Moore, Richard H. decd., Heirs	27	Patton, J.T., application for pension approved	90
Moore, Thomas L.	27	Patton, Ludwell F., application for aid approved	79
		Patton, Ludwell F., exemption from taxes	82
		Payne, Arthur M.	6
		Payne, Daniel	6
		Payne, James	9

Surname Given Name	Page	Surname Given Name	Page
Rixey, Mary (Thomas) decd., Heirs	15	Sanders, Mary M., application for pension approved	90
Rixey, Presley M.	15	Sanford, Agnes (Preston)	29
Rixey, Samuel	15	Sanford, Luther M. decd., Heirs	38
Rixey, Samuel (son of Samuel)	15	Sanford, Meredith	66
Roach, James M.	12	Sanford, Sarah Ann (Kernes)	66
Roach, John R.	12	Saunders, Caroline (Davis)	14
Roach, Juliet (Claggett)	10	Saunders, Thompson	14
Roach, Patty (Rev. War Pensioner); Heirs	12	Scott, Fanny (Payne)	6
Roach, Patty decd., (widow of John); death certified	12	Scott, John (commander of Black Horse Troop as patrol)	41
Roach, Robert	10, 12.	Scott, R.	65
Roach, Thomas C.	12	Scott, R Taylor	75
Robertson, H.H.	57, 60.	Scott, R. Taylor, decd., Resolutions at his death	82-84.
Robinson, George C., application for aid approved	80	Scott, Robert	63
Robinson, George H., application for commutation	75-76.	Scott, Robert E., decd., Notice of Resolution at his death	54
Roe, Bernard (son of John)	11	Sealock, George R., application for aid approved	87
Roe, Bernard decd., No Heirs	10	Seaton, George L. (a.k.a. George Ludwell)	62
Roe, Catherine	11	Settle, Nancy (Jett)	16
Roe, Henry decd., Heirs	10	Seymour, Selina E. (Luckett)	20
Roe, Henry F.	11	Shaw, Elizabeth (Burk)	7
Roe, James	11	Shaw, J.N., application for commutation	70
Roe, John	10	Shirley, J.R., application for pension approved	90
Roe, Nancy	11	Shumate, Lewis	55
Roe, Sarah (dau. of John)	11	Shutts, Ann E.	5
Roe, Wm. decd., (Surg. Mate, VSN); Heirs	10	Shutts, Samuel	5
Roe, Winifred	11	Simpson, Sophia (Claggett)	10
Rogers, Frances C. (Jett)	16	Simpson, Thomas	10
Rogers, James	58, 64.	Skinker, Harriet (Keith)	36
Rogers, Mary M. (Jett)	16		
Rutherford, Mary Ann, application for aid approved	80		

Surname Given Name	Page
Wiser, Nelly (widow of Michael)	8
Wiser, Thomas decd., (1812); BLW Claim	39
Wiser, Thomas decd., (1812); death certified; Heirs	38
Withers, Alexander S.	1
Withers, Andrew F.	1
Withers, Edward B.	1
Withers, Elizabeth S.	1
Withers, Enoch K. (Rev. War Officer); Heirs	1
Withers, Horatio C.	1
Withers, Jane	1
Withers, Jesse (US Pensioner); death certified	1
Withers, Jesse H.	1
Withers, Margaret (Farrow)	17
Withers, Susan E. M.	1
Withers, Thomas T.	5
Withers, Thomas T. (son of Enoch K.)	1
Wood, Sallie M., application for pension approved	90
Woodward, Polly Ann, application for aid approved	81
Wright, James (Captain, Va. Cont. Line); Heirs	39
Young, Mary (BLW Claim)	12

www.ingramcontent.com/pod-product-compliance
Lightning Source LLC
Chambersburg PA
CBHW052114090426
42741CB00009B/1811